TRUMP'S RETURN

Publisher & Coeditor-in-Chief Deborah Chasman

Coeditor-in-Chief Joshua Cohen

Executive Editor Matt Lord

Associate Editor Cameron Avery

Associate Publisher Jasmine Parmley

Circulation Manager Irina Costache

Contributing Editors Thomas Ferguson, Adom Getachew, Lily Hu, Walter Johnson, Robin D. G. Kelley, Paul Pierson, Becca Rothfeld, & Simon Torracinta

Production Assistant Ione Barrows

Editorial Assistant Harrison Knight

Finance Manager Anthony DeMusis III

Board of Advisors Derek Schrier (Chair), Margo Beth Fleming, Archon Fung, Deborah Fung, Larry Kramer, Richard M. Locke, Jeff Mayersohn, Scott Nielsen, Robert Pollin, Hiram Samel, Kim Malone Scott, Brandon M. Terry, & Michael Voss

Interior Graphic Design Zak Jensen & Alex Camlin

Cover Design Alex Camlin

Trump's Return is *Boston Review* issue 2025.1 (Forum 33 / 50.1 under former designation system).

Image on page 42: Reuters

Printed and bound in the United States by Sheridan.

Distributed by Haymarket Books (www.haymarketbooks.org) to the trade in the U.S. through Consortium Book Sales and Distribution (www.cbsd.com) and internationally through Ingram Publisher Services International (www.ingramcontent.com).

To become a member, visit bostonreview.net/memberships.

For questions about donations and major gifts, contact Irina Costache, irina@bostonreview.net.

For questions about memberships, email members@bostonreview.net.

Boston Review
PO Box 390568
Cambridge, MA 02139

ISSN: 0734-2306 / ISBN: 978-1-946511-93-5

Authors retain copyright of their work.
© 2025, Boston Critic, Inc.

CONTENTS

Editors' Note — 5

The New MAGA Coalition | ESSAY — 8
David Austin Walsh

Blood Ties | ESSAY — 20
Jeanne Morefield

ELECTION CHRONICLES

    On Fighting Back — 43
    Robin D. G. Kelley

    On Buying Elections — 53
    Mark Schmitt

    On Rebuilding Labor — 62
    Janice Fine & Benjamin Schlesinger

    On the Imperial Boomerang — 69
    Noura Erakat

    On a Real Post-Neoliberal Agenda — 81
    Marshall Steinbaum

How to Build a Workers' Party | REVIEW — 97
Gianpaolo Baiocchi

The Parenting Panic | REVIEW   112
Aaron Bady

Syria's "Human Debris" | ESSAY   135
Joelle M. Abi-Rached

The Reality of Settler Colonialism | REVIEW   151
Samuel Hayim Brody

CONTRIBUTORS   175

EDITORS' NOTE

DONALD TRUMP IS back in the White House. His campaign claims—immigrants are stealing, murdering, and collecting public benefits; the United States is a hapless victim of other countries' treachery—are not true. But they are powerful. This issue demystifies them and imagines a path forward.

David Austin Walsh examines Trump's coalition of America First nationalists and Silicon Valley billionaires. These diverse interests have thus far successfully united around opposition to "wokeness," much as the specter of communism bound the old "fusionism" of social and economic conservatives. Whether these fractious alliances will hold remains to be seen.

Jeanne Morefield takes a longer view. What explains the appeal of Trump's immigrant "invasion" story, now codified by executive order? She blames an exceptionalism decades in the making, embraced by "every mainstream narrative about American politics—Democratic and Republican, liberal and reactionary." Focusing on the border obscures the role of Big Pharma in creating our fentanyl crisis. And it erases the principal cause of American pain: our particular brand of racial capitalism that makes life in the United States fundamentally different from life in every other wealthy nation in the world.

Our Election Chronicles further illuminate the consequences of this exceptionalism: the staggering scale of money in politics, and the difficulty of reducing it through any flavor of campaign finance reform; organized labor's disconnect from the lives of so many working people; the link between U.S.-backed violence in Gaza and political repression at home; and the Democrats' momentous failure to rein in inequality. Confronting these obstacles, Robin D. G. Kelley argues, requires a movement with the power "to dispel ruling-class lies about how our economy and society actually work."

What does that look like? In his review of Adam Kirsch's *On Settler Colonialism*, Samuel Hayim Brody identifies the sleight of hand that characterizes so much of our public discourse. Rather than engaging an idea, Kirsch tries to make it disappear. We must instead take movements for justice seriously.

Gianpaolo Baiocchi shows what that can achieve. Reviewing a new biography, he takes inspiration from the extraordinary rise of Lula, who founded a workers' party as a young metalworker and is now serving a third term as Brazil's president after defeating Trump ally Jair Bolsonaro. Baiocchi credits the movement's success to Lula's ability to "speak plainly to the needs of ordinary working people" and "articulate a progressive, pro-democracy project in a way that always broadens the umbrella." His lesson for this moment: "opposition parties need something more than a technocratic defense of the status quo."

Inauguration Day at the U.S. Capitol. Image: Getty Images

THE NEW MAGA COALITION
David Austin Walsh

THE LINEUP at Donald Trump's second inaugural was a veritable billionaires' row, with the heaviest hitters of Big Tech out in full force. Elon Musk, the world's richest man and incoming head of Trump's new Department of Government Efficiency (DOGE), treated the crowd to what sure seemed to be a Nazi salute. Amazon CEO Jeff Bezos, Meta CEO Mark Zuckerberg, Google CEO Sundar Pichai, and Apple CEO Tim Cook stood near him as Trump was sworn in. Meanwhile Vivek Ramaswamy, initially tapped as Musk's partner at DOGE and now reportedly being pushed out of the Trump world altogether, stood near the back.

The new tech right has taken advantage of the moment to lambast its cultural enemies. Zuckerberg went on Joe Rogan's podcast days before the inauguration to complain about his overly woke workforce, lament that society has been "neutered," insist that companies need more "masculine energy," and defend his decision to abolish fact checking and hate speech management on Facebook and Instagram.

Along with more stalwart tech right luminaries Peter Thiel and Marc Andreessen, Zuckerberg and Bezos have spent the better part of the interregnum between the election and the inauguration shamelessly flattering Trump. This was surely done not just to keep federal dollars flowing to their businesses—for all the talk of Silicon Valley's libertarian ethos, Big Tech has always heavily relied on government contracts and subsidies—but also because Trump is, for all intents and purposes, one of them: a billionaire who, insofar as he can be said to have real political views at all, believes in the untrammeled power of the boss.

So why has fellow billionaire Ramaswamy been sidelined, despite serving as one of Trump's biggest backers and surrogates last year in the wake of his own failed presidential run? The day after Christmas, he waded into a social media firestorm over the H-1B visa system, tweeting that American culture has "venerated mediocrity over excellence" and celebrates the "jock over the valedictorian." That's why, he said, Big Tech must bring in workers from overseas. Unsurprisingly, the subtext—that native-born American workers are lazy, mediocre, and entitled—drew considerable opprobrium from other elements of Trump's coalition. The nativist "America First" base, with a nontrivial number of avowed white nationalists in its ranks, is not the most receptive audience for a Thomas Friedman–style "The World Is Flat" lecture about American workers falling short against Indian and Chinese labor.

Far-right influencer Laura Loomer, who prompted the whole visa meltdown by criticizing Trump's appointment of Sriram Krishnan as AI czar, spent the better part of a week tearing into Ramaswamy and other defenders of the program—including Musk (who wrote that he would "go to war on this issue the likes of which you cannot possibly comprehend") and eventually Trump himself (who called it a "great program"). This was the first major public split in MAGA world since Trump's election, and its ferocity raises questions about the durability of the coalition. What do these fractures portend? Can MAGA survive in power?

GIVEN THE MISHMASH of various interests, there is certainly potential for enduring crackups. The crude Kremlinology of inaugural seating seems to indicate that not only do Big Tech's tycoons consider Trump's win their doing, but that Trump himself seems to feel similarly—and yet Musk had no qualms publicly criticizing Trump's "Stargate" AI venture the day it was announced. At the same time, the nativist and white nationalist right has long been a stable of fervent Trump support, a faction to whom he and his surrogates actively cater. The brazen and undisguised racism toward Haitian immigrants; the campaign's capstone rally at Madison Square Garden in October, featuring disturbing speeches from Tucker Carlson and the comedian Tony Hinchcliffe; and, of course, the proposals to deport up to 15 million people from the United States—all are testament to the strength of this prong in the Trump coalition.

There are also other, less pronounced interests in the mix. Organized labor can hardly be considered to be a key constituency on the right, but Teamsters president Sean O'Brien's refusal to endorse

Harris—and his speech at the Republican National Convention in July—did manage to wring the nomination of Congresswoman Lori Chavez-DeRemer for head of the Department of Labor. (In 2023 she was one of only three Republicans in the House to cosponsor the proposed Protecting the Right to Organize Act.) These concessions to the conservative wing of labor are at odds with Silicon Valley; the Teamsters have invested a considerable amount of time, energy, and resources in organizing Amazon warehouses, and Big Tech has made no secret of its hostility to unionization efforts. Then there are other industrial interests in Trump's coalition—he made a point of praising American manufacturing in his inaugural address, pledging to "revoke the electric vehicle mandate" (despite Musk owning the most highly valued electric vehicle manufacturing company in the world), and of course he retains the traditional support of Republicans from Wall Street.

How did these various groups become part of a big(ish)-tent coalition in the first place? The answer is "woke."

During the Cold War, anticommunism served as the glue that held conflicting elements of the right together. The populist and conspiracist John Birch Society, the traditionalists in the Southern Agrarian school, the renegade ex-Trotskyists in the *National Review* orbit, and the libertarian cultists around Ayn Rand all shared a fundamental opposition to communism, both at home and abroad. The whole point of conservative "fusionism" was to combine the traditionalism and social conservatism of the old Burkean right (and its descendants in twentieth-century Protestant and Catholic thought) with market capitalism to oppose communism. "Communism" itself was a slippery term for this set, often bearing little relation to the realities of the Soviet Union or Communist China—or, for that matter, what left-wing radicals in the United States preached or practiced. Rather, the word was a catch-all specter that could variously connote the ravages of state planning, the anarchism of street protests, or the godlessness of modern secular society—not an empty vessel, exactly, but a foil and common enemy against which a political coalition of often diametrically opposed interests could congeal.

"Wokeness" has done the same work for various right-wing factions in the 2020s, providing a way to classify and delegitimize all sorts of actors. Don't like immigrants? It's woke leftists who want to open the borders! Don't like not being able to say racist and sexist slurs at work? It's the fault of the wokes! Don't like some of the directions organized labor has taken, especially under the leadership of Shawn Fain? It's because the UAW has been taken over by woke grad students! As the Manhattan Institute's Christopher Rufo—one of this strategy's principal architects—has made explicit, anti-wokeness became the essential element in a right-wing war of position: an easy way to signal a whole host of political, educational, and class views, to recruit a heterogeneous coalition beyond the traditional base of the GOP, and to stoke infighting among liberals and the left.

The problem for this strategy going forward is that anti-wokeness as a political force is now effectively spent. For one thing, there's likely to be less widespread rhetoric of the sort that the right might so successfully tar and feather as "woke." Those parts of the left that weren't already opposed to corporate-friendly identity politics from the get-go broke with it years ago; the Democratic establishment appears to have turned decisively against it as well, embracing the specious claims of centrist pundits like Matt Yglesias, Adam Jentleson, and Jonathan Chait that Democratic concessions to "the groups"—progressive advocacy organizations composed of highly educated multicultural elites—are the main reason for Kamala Harris's defeat. And now the right itself has ridden the wave of anti-woke panic into power over all three branches of government. Without the common enemy of "wokeness" (however real or imagined) binding various factions together, we can expect more fissures.

That is not to say it's all going to fall apart on a dime. Ramaswamy, for his part, may not be permanently exiled, despite the white nationalist outcry; Trump has proposed that he serve out J. D. Vance's Senate term in Ohio. Besides, the tech right's ideology—its eugenicist thinking, its defense of elite power and privilege, and its just-so stories about the power of entrepreneurship and capitalism—resonates with Trump's deeply ingrained beliefs about himself as a "winner." A few years ago the writer John Ganz somewhat cheekily proposed a dichotomy between "nerd fascism" and "jock fascism"—the weird Silicon Valley engineers re-upping race and IQ science versus the id of the average American cop and petit bourgeois business owner. Trump appealed to both factions while himself remaining quintessentially a jock, but Vance's ascendancy signals growing power for a nerd-jock synthesis.

Though the details of Vance's biography are now well known, the influence of Yale Law School professor Amy Chua on his career cannot be overstated. Most famous for her book *Battle Hymn of the Tiger Mother*, Chua encouraged Vance to write his breakthrough memoir *Hillbilly Elegy*. She also coauthored—with her husband, fellow Yale Law School professor Jed Rubenfeld—the 2014 book *The Triple Package*, which offered a cultural explanation for certain ethnic groups' successes in America. The book gave the patina of elite academic respectability to the preexisting attitudes of much of the new (and ethnically diverse) tech right elite; as sociologist Steve Steinberg wrote in these pages, it was a tool designed to "provide indispensable legitimacy for social class hierarchy." Of course, cultural pathology has been the preferred conservative explanation for Black poverty dating back to the Moynihan Report; Chua and Rubenfeld were tapping an oft-used well. What was novel in the 2010s was that the kind of argument they made began to be deployed by the right against the group it had traditionally defended: poor whites. Kevin Williamson wrote an influential *National Review* cover story in 2016 using this precise language, and three months later it was elaborated as the primary thesis of Vance's memoir.

It was a short step from here to Silicon Valley, where Vance moved after two years in law to work as a venture capitalist, including a stint at Thiel's firm. But since embracing MAGAism after 2020 he has shifted his rhetoric. His speech at the RNC last year was full of paeans to the American working class, and he led the way during the campaign with the most bigoted rhetoric about Haitian immigrants. At the same time, he has notably been silent about H-1B visas and Ramaswamy's tweets. There are certainly elements of sheer opportunism here, but if there is going to be a synthesis between the tech right and America First, Vance will likely be its linchpin.

Some signs of what this might look like are already taking shape in a kind of delicate balancing act: throw a bone to the tech right here (say, H-1B visas), then to America First nationalists there. The latter may be the junior partner in this dance—and how long this can go on remains to be seen—but it's not going to lose every time. On the first two days of his new administration Trump issued a flurry of executive orders—many not simply red meat for his base, like renaming the Gulf of Mexico the "Gulf of America," but real policy victories for the America First right, including several on immigration. Another such win is the confirmation of former Fox News personality Pete Hegseth as Secretary of Defense. Hegseth is obviously an unhinged monster—he has been credibly accused of multiple sexual assaults—but more significantly, he is a fixture in far-right political circles. Not unlike Vance, he has some intellectual bonafides, writing his senior thesis at Princeton in 2003 on "Modern Presidential Rhetoric and the Cold War Context" supervised by Patrick Deneen, one of the most prominent postliberal thinkers on the Catholic right (whom Vance, himself a Catholic convert, has also cited as an influence).

Hegseth's own politics are probably best described as Christian nationalist, an ideology ultimately derived from the fascistic forms of Protestantism pioneered by figures like Gerald L. K. Smith in the 1930s and 1940s. His installment as head of the Department of Defense—the largest executive department in terms of both budget and personnel, and the very heart of global empire—is a sign that Trump's support for the America First side of his coalition still matters politically.

ALL OF WHICH leads us to the fascism question. Sociologist Dylan Riley has argued that Trumpism could not be considered meaningfully fascistic—at least in the Marxist sense of the term—because it lacked certain essential features of twentieth-century fascism, above all the foil of a powerful and well-organized left threatening political revolution in a period of structural crisis. While Riley's arguments can be critiqued on their own terms—historian Joseph Fronczak counters that "the left" only became recognizable through *anti*-fascism in the 1920s and 1930s—they also fail to account for the political strength of left-wing protest movements in the 2010s.

The fact that Occupy Wall Street, Black Lives Matter, and #MeToo failed to fundamentally change American political economy, end or significantly curtail the carceral state, and usher in a durable and expansive sea change against misogyny and sexual violence should not blind us to the reality that left protest movements really were substantively setting the cultural and political agenda during the first Trump administration. There really were tens of thousands—if not hundreds of thousands—of people engaged in radical political action during the George Floyd uprisings. And there really were countless liberals in a variety of social institutions, from business to corporate media to the academy, who responded to these movements with a welter of rhetoric and initiatives—including an intensification of administrative diversity, equity, and inclusion efforts. In short, the right's hysteria about DEI—and before DEI "critical race theory," and before critical race theory "cultural Marxism"—did have some basis in reality, which is to say that for a time a particular form of liberal identity politics really did exert meaningful power throughout American culture.

This is not at all to say that the Democrats have been a revolutionary political force. The point is that a cultural revolution of sorts did take place in American social life, and all this was absolutely terrifying to the right. It is no coincidence that the Proud Boys emerged as the de facto street-fighting wing of MAGA during the first Trump administration—engaging in long-running battles with organized left-wing protesters in Portland, winning Trump's endorsement during one of the 2020 presidential debates, and participating in the January 6 coup attempt. Nor is it a coincidence that the United States saw a spate of white nationalist mass shootings during Trump's first term, or for that matter that right-wing vigilantes—Kyle Rittenhouse most prominently—were feted as heroes for fighting back against lawless radicalism. Biden rode into office on a wave of outrage at all this, but under his administration Democrats squandered the radical potential of the protest moment, capturing an elite form of the identity politics groundswell and failing to deliver transformative change. Unsurprisingly, Harris's electoral strategy—offering, besides a strong message on abortion, little more than empty rhetoric against an avowedly "existential" threat—disaffected and demobilized both liberals and the left, whose turnout plummeted in November.

Resistance liberalism was thus at last decisively revealed to be a politically bankrupt ideology, incapable of achieving its foundational goal: keeping Trump out of the White House. In 2016, Trump's surprise victory in the Electoral College—combined with his loss of the popular vote by nearly three million—sparked spontaneous protests and a flurry of organizing among liberals. The predominant mood among them today is quite different: bitter resignation, if not outright obedience. Many ordinary citizens are organizing, especially at local levels, but there have been no mass protests comparable to those of four years ago. And various liberal institutions have already signaled their capitulation to the new order. Establishment voices like MSNBC's Joe Scarborough and Mika Brzezinski—who were calling Trump a fascist and comparing him to Hitler just two months ago—are now patting themselves on the back for ensuring an orderly transition of power. Meanwhile, the left's only serious threat to liberal political hegemony was effectively defanged with Bernie Sanders's defeat in the 2020 Democratic primary.

Two factors now stand in the way of 2016/2017 Popular Front–style mobilization. One is that this time Trump won the popular vote (though just shy of winning a majority); no one can dispute that he was the legitimate choice of the American people in a free and fair election. The other is Gaza. Israel/Palestine has long been a wedge between liberals and leftists—the Women's March, the largest organized protest movement in American history, was effectively dissolved because of infighting over this issue—but the salience and intensity has escalated exponentially since the October 7 attacks and Israel's subsequent genocidal campaign. The left already mobilized its (relatively feeble) strength in 2024 in protest against the Biden administration's unconditional support for Israel; not only were its demands ignored, but liberal administrators at colleges and universities around the country—as well as Democratic elected officials—sent in riot cops to beat student and faculty protesters. Forging an anti-Trump popular coalition between a deflated and demoralized liberalism and a left that has spent the better part of a year on the receiving end of liberal repression is, at least at the moment, effectively impossible.

With political opposition to MAGAism at its organizational and cultural nadir, there is simply no need in 2025 for the fascist extra that Riley said was missing. The greatest fear of institutional liberalism in the 2010s was that Trump would be "normalized," which meant effectively that the movement he stands for would be deemed politically legitimate and absorbed into the apparatus of the American state without opposition or protest. That has now happened. And that means the Proud Boys are now superfluous. The mass pardons of the January 6 insurrectionists, while odious, are unlikely to catalyze a new wave of organized paramilitarism. When the forces of capital come to the inauguration to bend the knee to the new political order, and the wealthiest man in the world can casually toss off a Nazi salute to a cheering crowd, the street fighters are no longer necessary.

BLOOD TIES
Jeanne Morefield

"They let—I think the real number is fifteen, sixteen million people into our country," Donald Trump told a crowd in December 2023 before stumbling into language that sounded more ominous than usual. "When they do that, we got a lot of work to do. They're poisoning the blood of our country."

When he had first tried out the language three months earlier, the Biden administration and other liberals were quick to point out the resonances with Hitler. "It seemed as if a perpetual stream of poison was being sent by some mysterious power to the very uttermost blood-vessels of what had once been a hero's body and was crippling common sense and the simple instinct of self-preservation more and more," the would-be Führer wrote of Germany in 1925. Trump would have none of it. "I never read *Mein Kampf*," he sputtered at a rally in Waterloo, Iowa, doubling down on the metaphor. Illegal immigrants, he insisted, "are destroying the blood of our country, they're destroying the fabric of our country." Soon after, J. D. Vance swooped to Trump's defense. "First of all," said Vance, "he didn't say immigrants were poisoning the blood of this country. He said illegal immigrants were poisoning the blood of this country, which is objectively and obviously true to anybody who looks at the statistics about fentanyl overdoses."

Vance's excuse is neat: cause meets effect and the blood is poisoned. In this story, illegal immigrants are "obviously and objectively" linked to the fentanyl overdoses that so many Americans have now experienced, personally or from a distance. The story is at once tautological, resistant to evidence—89 percent of apprehended fentanyl traffickers are American citizens, and the majority of fentanyl crosses the border at legal ports of entry—and unidirectional. It begins with Chinese labs and flows through the southern border, carried on the bodies of Mexican illegal immigrants, invading and wrecking the bodies of innocent American sons and daughters.

This invasion story, which Trump codified by executive order on the first day of his second term, echoes other body-snatching narratives today—the border is a "child trafficking delivery service"; migrants bring "very contagious diseases"; a parasitic worm eats away at the brain of Trump's pledged nominee for director of Health and Human Services—but the opioid crisis feels singularly cruel in its grip upon the body politic. Driven by a spike in fentanyl consumption over the last several years, drug overdose deaths increased by 50 percent in the United States between 2019 and 2021. According to the Centers for Disease Control and Prevention, nearly 109,000 people died of drug overdoses in 2022 alone, and overdoses by synthetic opioids are likely now the leading cause of death for Americans aged 18 to 45.

Last July, in response to these terrifying statistics, the Biden administration announced new policies "to counter the scourge of fentanyl and other synthetic drugs," actions that start with the "442 million potentially lethal doses of fentanyl . . . seized at U.S. borders." Chief among these proposed policies: a promise "to invest in detection technology" and add "dozens of new inspection systems" to the U.S. border regime. While increasing detection technologies and inspection systems at legal points of entry might in fact be necessary at this point, the Biden-Harris scheme also reiterates the longstanding orientation toward drug policy adopted by Democrats and Republicans alike: it assumes that the problem begins and ends at the border. In this, the focus of the proposal mirrors Barack Obama's National Southwest Border Counternarcotics Strategy (released in 2009), George W. Bush's Operation Jump Start (launched in 2006), and goal four of Bill Clinton's National Drug Control Strategy (announced in 1997): to "shield America's air, land, and sea frontier from the drug threat."

In other words, the stage for Trump's particularly bloody equation of the border with the fentanyl crisis was set long ago. He needs no Hitlerian inspiration for his rhetoric; both Democrats and Republicans have been building this common sense for years, renovating and expanding its capacities over time—including with bids for ever more border patrol agents, counterinsurgency funding, and technology. According to this homegrown conventional wisdom, "lethal doses" of drugs flow in a single direction: from the outside in. They are never "of us" or "from us." When Trump began linking fentanyl to immigrants in 2016, he simply moved into the house built by his predecessors, amped up the vitriol, and promised to stop the invasion.

This time around, Trump says, the war must be brought to Mexico itself. He assured us he would target drug cartels as foreign terrorist organizations—and already started that process by executive order. He says he will order the Pentagon "to make appropriate use of special forces, cyber warfare, and other covert and overt actions to inflict maximum damage on cartel leadership, infrastructure, and operations." He promises to deploy the Navy to impose a blockade, pass legislation to ensure that drug smugglers receive the death penalty, invoke the Alien Enemies Act of 1798 to deport drug dealers, and end birthright citizenship. The question, a senior Trump transition member told *Rolling Stone*, is not *if* the United States should invade Mexico, but "how much." As crusader and new Secretary of Defense Pete Hegseth might intone, this time the blood of the infidels must be spilled to protect the blood of the lamb.

THE BEAUTIFUL BOY is hunched over on a park bench jamming the burrito I've just bought him into his mouth. He is all shades of grey. Grey sweatshirt and sweatpants that hang off his once-bulky body like a moldy blanket. Grey feet, poking out ashy, from the tips of his grey flip-flops. Grey, skittish face that chews and cries and sniffs and stares. When he talks about the maggots in the food, the violent dealer, the multiple overdoses, his voice stays flat. Grey. As if to match the palette. When he shuffles off the park bench beside me, I wonder—as I do multiple times a day and several times (upright, with a "bang!" in my head) in the middle of the night—if this is the hour the beautiful Boy goes home, falls asleep, and never wakes up.

He smokes his fentanyl, no need for injections. The messiness of heroin, with its elaborate, needle-ridden ritual, seems quaint by comparison. Except for plasma donation, and the occasional punch in the nose, this is a bold new blood-free universe. And in this universe, where he is almost always dying, I am almost always cracked in two. I am shattered. Raw. I want, need, a story that connects cause to effect. I want—need—to find the monster that clawed inside him and stab it to death. I want—I need—a straight line that ends in salvation. Or in answers. Or at the very least, revenge. I crave blood.

IN THE EARLY 1990s, when Richard Sackler and Purdue Pharma set out to make OxyContin the best-selling pain medication of all time, they were also thinking about blood. Specifically, about the fact that the only thing that distinguished their new drug from run-of-the-mill Oxycodone—and thus, from run-of-the-mill heroin—was a time-release coating that allowed it to dissolve over a supposedly twelve-hour period into the bloodstream. OxyContin's meteoric commercial success was entirely the product of Purdue's uniquely aggressive marketing strategy, which originally targeted some of the most economically decimated regions of the country and poured millions of dollars into speaker's fees, free lunches, and other forms of compensation for doctors. Ultimately the goal was to get physicians to prescribe opioids and downplay the possibility of addiction. The time-release coating, sales reps assured everyone, kept the drip of opioid to a trickle.

As we now know, this privately held company understood full well that the product it was peddling was a highly addictive "nuclear weapon" of a narcotic. Purdue knew that its coating was porous and that each dose did not last twelve hours. It was also aware, from its own data and from reports by its sales reps, that OxyContin was being widely abused. And yet, Purdue not only continued to expand sales; it started a program of free samples. In 1996, the year OxyContin went on the market, the company brought in $48 million in revenue. By 2010 it was making $3 billion annually. That same year, the company finally introduced a tamper-proof, crush-proof coating to discourage abuse, but the damage was done. Deaths by opioid overdoses in the United States had nearly quadrupled since 1999, and millions of people had developed crippling addictions. The foundation was laid for a heroin epidemic, creating a ready-made market for the much more powerful, much cheaper synthetic opioid that appeared on the scene: fentanyl.

It is tempting to lay the blame for this crisis squarely at the feet of the Sackler family and Purdue Pharma. After all, doing so reverses the one-way narrative of the alien invasion story, transforming the epidemic into a homegrown problem of corporate greed in the heartland. And yet, this story is only partially satisfying. While it may explain the American origins of this crisis, it fails to explain why this crisis is so uniquely American—why statistics on opioid addiction and death in this country continue to dwarf figures from any other wealthy nation. Indeed the United States has the highest rate of overdose deaths in the world, a figure that has remained constant throughout the early 2020s even as other countries have seen decreases. Even the singular rapaciousness of the Sacklers cannot explain the singular hold of opioids on America.

For that, you have to look at what makes life in the United States fundamentally different from life in every other wealthy nation in the world: its lack of a universal, publicly funded health care system and even a modest social safety net. Countries with functioning social support programs do not see such radically high levels of economic precarity and homelessness—conditions that significantly increase the likelihood of turning to drugs. And countries with universal, publicly funded health care have a markedly different relationship with the pharmaceutical industry because governments in these countries have an incentive to use consolidated negotiating power to bargain with drug companies over prices.

Not only does this incentive not exist in the United States; the financial ecosystem surrounding the for-profit health care industry works in tandem with a weak regulatory structure, permissive marketing laws, and a highly decentralized system of oversight that makes individual doctors more susceptible to direct manipulation by pharmaceutical companies. In an environment in which doctors measure consultations with patients in minutes, and where so much basic health care takes place in the high-pressure environment of the emergency room, it is often easier to simply write a prescription than devote the time to discuss pain management. To add insult to injury, despite U.S. health care costs accounting for 17.6 percent of GDP (higher than any other country in the world), around 8 percent of the population—some 26 million people—has no health insurance at all, while another 23 percent of the population is underinsured. To be uninsured or underinsured in the United States is to be one bad diagnosis away from financial ruin or homelessness. Ultimately, this means that Americans are both *more* susceptible to the economic factors associated with a higher likelihood of opioid addiction and, once addicted, *less* likely to have insurance to pay for treatment.

In short, it is Americans' exceptional exposure to capitalism that makes them exceptionally vulnerable to the opioid epidemic. And yet American exceptionalism also makes that fact so roundly impossible for anyone in the political establishment to acknowledge. Instead, for the last thirty years, a succession of Republican and Democratic politicians have focused—laserlike—on the border. Biden temporarily expanded the U.S. welfare state only to preside over its further contraction and vow to "address our broken immigration system." After having publicly backed away from her 2020 commitment to Medicare for All, Harris devoted barely a word of her 2024 campaign to health care, pledging, instead, to fund more agents, buy more drug detection equipment, and prosecute more traffickers.

Into this crackling vortex—where the fentanyl crisis and border militarization expand hand in hand—a crowd of fulminating reactionaries descends, whispering in your ear, then pounding on the table, raging that Biden has "the blood of American citizens on his hands." Into this vortex, Trump roars like the wrath of God, promising again and again to rain down fire and brimstone on these "bloodthirsty criminals" crossing the border in a tidal wave of contagion. Into this vortex—both preceding and responding to Trump like a frantic, proleptic chorus—descends a popular movement with a mystical, phantasmagoric vision of reality and a parallel story about cause and effect, in which Trump will save "thousands upon thousands" of children from the underground bunkers where the Clintons and a host of Democratic deep state operatives are holding them captive. Harvesting their adrenochrome. Draining their blood.

IN HIS 1933 classic, *The Mass Psychology of Fascism*, psychoanalyst, sociologist, and political economist Wilhelm Reich looked closely at fascism's conflation of racial purity and "blood poisoning" and concluded that one "does not render the cause of human freedom a service by merely deriding this mysticism instead of unmasking it." He went on to explain the affective appeal of fascism for what he later called the "broadest masses," whose support, he argued, had fueled the worst abuses—"predatory imperialism, exploitation of workers, racial suppression"—of the capitalist era.

Unmasking the enormously popular, QAnon-inflated conspiracy theory—now firmly established in the mainstream Republican Party—about a global cabal of vampiric, child-trafficking, deep state actors also requires attending to its mass affective appeal. Like the Nazi rhetoric that Reich analyzes, it is antisemitic in blood-libel form, if not precisely in content, and it overlaps substantially with the equally conspiratorial anti-vaccine movement that also gained momentum during the COVID-19 pandemic. One cannot appreciate the appeal of these views without recognizing them as funhouse mirrors, reflecting a twisted but not entirely invented version of American political reality. In their obsessions with the Clintons, at least, there is a tiny kernel of truth pulsing within the bizarre *Weltanschauung* of the conspiracy theorists, about the origins of the opioid crisis and the politics of the southern border.

When he was elected president in 1992, Bill Clinton was in the unique position of making two fundamentally transformative changes to both the national and the global economic and political landscape. First, he came in with a clear mandate to transform health care in America. Both Jesse Jackson's surprisingly successful primary campaign in 1988 and Harris Wofford's equally surprising senatorial election in 1991 suggested that there was widespread public support for ending the dysfunctional for-profit health care system. And yet, despite this mandate, both Bill and Hillary Clinton—who chaired the president's task force on health care reform—made it clear from the beginning that they were uninterested in a public solution.

Instead, the Clintons championed "managed care competition," the approach preferred by the insurance industry, in which private companies still exercised near total control over prices and health care providers. They ostracized supporters of single-payer and national health care from their deliberations. And they brought to Congress a hugely complicated bill that no one understood, which Republicans gleefully branded as socialist. President Clinton devoted the rest of his administration's work on health care to deregulating the pharmaceutical industry and weakening the Food and Drug Administration, both of which contributed substantially to the opioid crisis.

In one fell stroke, the Clintons thus transformed health care reform into the third rail of American policy issues and suppressed discussion of any meaningful change to the for-profit system for the next thirty years. Indeed, this fall, when Senator Elizabeth Warren attempted to draw attention to the outpouring of frustration and rage at the insurance industry following the murder of CEO Brian Thompson, she was forced to "clarify" her statements by a Democratic and Republic political establishment fixated on the moral question of violence and incapable of acknowledging just how bad the crisis in capitalist-driven health care had become.

Second, as commander in chief, Clinton had the unprecedented opportunity, and the mandate, to reconsider America's embrace of global primacy, the reigning foreign policy ideology in Washington since the end of World War II. As a worldview and a policy commitment, primacy aims to ensure that the United States remains the dominant military, economic, and political hegemon in the world, to integrate other states into U.S.-designed markets (by force if necessary), and to do so in a way that, in Patrick Porter's words, goes "well beyond what it minimally needs to defend or deter threats." Throughout the postwar period, the U.S. commitment to primacy has resulted in the expansion of America's military capacities (to over 750 military bases in 80 countries and more at-ready military personnel in more places than any other people, nation, or empire in history), multiple deadly wars, interference in the internal affairs of roughly fifty sovereign nations (that we know of), forced regime changes, assassinations, counterinsurgencies, and support for authoritarian, antidemocratic regimes throughout the world (including

Obama's support for the 2009 right-wing coup in Honduras, which has contributed substantially to the spike in Central American asylum seekers). At this point in America's history, maintaining global primacy requires that the federal government pour nearly a trillion dollars a year into its security budget.

While in office, Clinton could have taken the end of the Cold War as an opportunity to rethink America's relationship to its military and to the rest of the world, starting by redistributing the "peace dividend" in other ways. As with the Marshall Plan, he could have poured resources into the public sector of a struggling and transitioning Russian state. He could have reassessed America's role in NATO and the role of NATO more generally, worked with his counterparts to begin denuclearization, and redistribute America's security budget domestically toward public spending in health care, education, science, and the arts. This was a moment when it was possible to reimagine the global economy in broadly more equitable terms and to reorient toward a true internationalism in which the United States was one among equals rather than a hegemon constantly driven by the need to maintain its supremacy.

All of this was possible. None of this happened. Instead, Clinton chose to sanction reckless privatization and economic "shock therapy" in Russia, to studiously avoid talking about denuclearization, and, most importantly, to leave unchallenged the underlying policy faith in the necessity of America's total military, political, and economic power.

In both domestic and global arenas, whatever platitudes Clinton mouthed to his adoring Democratic fans about a more equitable world were ultimately overruled by his even stronger commitment to American capital. According to one study, at least fifteen of Clinton's key policymakers had direct ties to a total of forty-one corporations. The Clinton administration facilitated unprecedented and lucrative mergers among major corporations associated with the military-industrial complex, that congeries of defense companies that relies upon an unchecked flow of public money for their private profit. Rather than reconsider America's military spending, Clinton expanded it. In inflation-adjusted dollars, the administration spent roughly $30 billion more on defense in 1995 than Nixon did in 1975 during a period of Soviet expansionism. It was also equally committed to assuring "open and equal U.S. access to foreign markets" for the post–Cold War era. This was to be a "world of free trade," a world Clinton helped breathe into being when he signed the North American Free Trade Agreement (NAFTA) in 1993.

Through all this, in the course of eight years, the Clinton administration completed the reforms of the Reagan revolution and ushered in an era of neoliberal barbarism. In Mexico, the economic regime inaugurated by NAFTA has led directly to the loss of some two million agricultural jobs and a mass movement of Mexican workers toward the abusive *maquiladora* economy of the border. In this brave new world, Mexican nationals work in foreign-owned export manufacturing firms, producing cheap goods for American consumers at wages that rapidly fell below pre-NAFTA rates. As economic hopelessness has grown, the number of Mexicans immigrating to the United States has also grown exponentially. At the same time, the 1996 amendments to the Immigration and Nationality Act and other legislation Clinton signed that year have increasingly allowed for the criminalization of those immigrants, harsher penalties for unauthorized entry, and impossible standards for family unification–based amnesties.

And yet, even as access to legal immigration shrinks along America's southern border—even as the number of migrant dead and disappeared continues to grow and vigilantes join with law enforcement in Arizona and Texas to terrorize undocumented men, women, and children—the U.S. border regime finds creative ways to serve capital. Every year, the United States issues a number of time-limited, non-immigrant visitor visas to Mexicans, allowing them to cross into El Paso and other border towns. Many do so in order to "donate" plasma at commercial plasma centers. Once in these centers, men and women—including many *maquiladora* workers—are connected to plasmapheresis machines where blood is drained from their arms, usually in exchange for a $50 prepaid Visa card. Their plasma is then commingled with the plasma of millions of U.S. citizens and undocumented immigrants throughout the country—usually poor, often unhoused, and often, like the beautiful Boy, addicted to fentanyl—and transformed into $35 billion of market value for the American pharmaceutical industry.

THE STORY I tell about the beautiful Boy's origins begins at the border. With maternal blood.

His mother was arrested for low-level drug smuggling in the southwest corner of Texas while sitting in the passenger seat of a broken-down car, her dealer boyfriend at the wheel, a screaming toddler in the back seat. (The Child Protective Services files emphasize the disconnect between miles traveled and dearth of diapers.) Out on bail in a medium-sized West Texas town, her child in foster care, far but near (by Texas standards) from her home, and occasionally unhoused, she had a one-night stand with a man at a party and got pregnant. She never saw him again.

The beautiful Boy's mother lived her whole life on the southwest fringes of a state that has been described as "the global epicenter for mass incarceration," within a racist ecosystem of policing that sat (and still sits) cheek by jowl with an increasingly violent, cross-border drug-trafficking economy that grows exponentially in response to worsening economic conditions in Mexico and rising levels of addiction in the United States. The beautiful Boy's mother clearly participated in this economy. And she was also clearly its victim. One can't help but imagine that she understood herself to have very little control over anything that was happening to her at the time, that she bounced along on waves of addiction and waves of events in a sea of other people, other systems, and other forces that existed outside herself and the accidental fetus burrowing within.

Even twenty years ago, Texas's now near-total abortion ban was already well in the making, and access to abortion services was extraordinarily limited, especially for women in rural areas of the state. The state is currently ranked among the three worst states for access to maternal health care and has long had the highest proportion of citizens without health insurance in the United States—twice the national rate and five percentage points higher than the next worst state, Oklahoma. As with limited access to abortion, these are long-term trends in health care disparities—trends that would not exist if the United States had a public system of universal health care.

Throughout those early months of her pregnancy, the beautiful Boy's mother abused multiple substances. They leeched though the placental barrier, flowing along the blooded passage from mother to fetus, settling into the beautiful Boy's developing brain, reorienting what would be his future executive functioning—his perception of time, of cause and effect—rendering him susceptible to, among other challenges, addiction.

In a redemption fantasy I sometimes have when I am most crushed by helplessness, I find his mother the day after the party, and I physically interject myself between her mouth and the bottle. Her mouth and the pipe. Her arm and the needle. Somehow, by sheer force of will, I inspire force of will in her, and she throws away the bottle, pipe, or needle with a dramatic fling of her arm and rises to her feet, gripped with a newfound determination to live a sober life. Then, in my mind, I see an image of the beautiful–fetus–Boy stretching out in her womb, his glistening brain untouched, sucking clean blood from the umbilical cord. Like tea through a straw.

In the real version of the story, the beautiful Boy is born prematurely into a community with among Texas's highest rates of childhood poverty, childhood asthma, homicide, and opioid addiction. In the real version of the story, the beautiful Boy's chances were scrambled, from the pre-beginning, by the precarity of the world around him.

Of course, the deep background to this real and felt sense of precarity and helplessness in the face of external forces—the drug trade, racist law enforcement—is the history of Anglo settler occupation and violence that has long stalked this southern fringe of Texas. Since well before the Treaty of Guadalupe in 1848, when Mexico ceded 55 percent of its territory and recognized the Rio Grande as the new border with the United States, the Texas Rangers—half police, half armed gang—played a pivotal role in securing the region for white settlement, wresting land by force from indigenous people and Mexican ranchers alike and hunting down runaway slaves for good measure. During the Mexican Revolution in the second decade of the twentieth century, Rangers and white vigilantes intensified this violence, waging a campaign of racial terror along the Texas-Mexico border during which at least 500 Mexicans (some estimates are as high as 5,000) were shot, lynched, or executed without trial. The decade reached its bloody zenith in 1918 with the massacre of nearly all the men and boys in the border town of Porvenir. Among Mexicans and Tejanos, the decade came to be known as *La Hora de Sangre*: The Hour of Blood.

At the core of this campaign of racial violence was white ranchers' and settlers' intolerance for Mexican and indigenous control of the land. But it was also driven by anxieties about land redistribution—specifically, the expropriation of wealthy *hacendado* land for Mexican peasants under the banner of figures like Emiliano Zapata. The idea appealed to small landholders and agrarian radicals on the American side of the border, too. From this perspective, La Hora de Sangre resembles what W. E. B. Du Bois describes in *Black Reconstruction* as the "counter-revolution of property." Writing on the post–Civil War South, Du Bois saw that an alliance was forged between northern industrialists, Southern oligarchs, and white peasants to prevent Black freedmen and white laborers from joining forces. The coalition of interests that ultimately came together in Texas to enforce the "white man's west" for white settler and white capitalist expansion served much the same purpose.

In his recent book *Late Fascism*, Alberto Toscano draws on the insights of Du Bois and other Black radical thinkers—George Padmore, Aimé Césaire, and Angela Davis among them—to highlight the constancy of this "counter-revolutionary" racial violence against subaltern populations both within and at the fringes of "actually existing liberal democracies"—in the colonies, in the prisons, along the borders. This violence, Toscano argues, is integral to the process by which settler and colonial capitalist democracies sustain themselves. An anti-fascist political consciousness, he concludes, must recognize the link between these everyday practices and the emergence of mass movements, reactionary and resentful, oriented toward purging the body politic of leftist poison.

At these historical junctures, the braided relationship between capitalism, liberal democracy, and fascism bursts through the color line. Some deep inkling of a real threat against "the people" by elites—today, an American opioid epidemic, forged in the bowels of the American pharmaceutical industry—peeks above the waves but quickly coils back into itself, transformed through conspiracy theory and the racist logic of the historical present into a revanchist politics foaming at the mouth for impure blood. The low thrum of racial containment resonating all around us all the time suddenly fills the air with the clamorous scream of a mighty, apocalyptic chorus. Meanwhile, as

Césaire put it in his 1950 classic, *Discourse on Colonialism*, the "very distinguished, very humanistic" bourgeois looks around, aghast, and discovers he "has a Hitler inside him."

Historically, as with our current situation, such moments have revealed both the fragility of liberal "democratic" institutions and their naked affiliations with racial power. In 1919, when the only Tejano member of the Texas legislature, José Tomás Canales, led a formal investigation into violent policing practices during La Hora de Sangre and brought nineteen charges against the Rangers, he was quickly confronted with the limitations of Texas's democratic system. During hearings in which he submitted evidence regarding the massacre in Porvenir and questioned witnesses, Canales was himself cross-examined by the lawyer for the Rangers. "Now, Mr. Canales," the attorney queried, "you are by blood a Mexican are you not?" "I am not a Mexican," a startled Canales replied. "I am an American citizen." The lawyer's follow-up question was short and to the point. "By blood?"

IN 1987, four years before he was diagnosed with the blood cancer that would ultimately take his life, Edward Said gave a lecture entitled "Representing the Colonized: Anthropology's Interlocutors" in which he laid out the critical orientation that guided both his academic and political writing. "When we consider the connections between the United States and the rest of the world," he insisted, "we are so to speak *of* the connections, not outside and beyond them." Aimed in part at researchers in the American academy, Said's words encouraged a dramatic methodological shift, away from presuming the neutrality of the observing subject who also happens to be living in an empire.

Politically, this reorientation begins at the point of overlap between American imperial power and American exceptionalism. For Said, who devoted so much of his life's work to making the question of Palestine visible for a world committed to its invisibility, being *of* the connections required recognizing the convergence between the destabilizing actions of the United States in the Middle East and the domestic narratives that rationalized these actions. By Said's lights, fighting to make Palestine visible, and for the right of Palestinians to narrate their own experience, began at sites of connection—the border, the refugee camp, the exiled individual, the prison, the military installation, the occupied territory—and then sought to reconnect the past to the present, American foreign policy to Palestine, domination to resistance, the outside to the inside, and the practice of American imperialism to the common sense of American exceptionalism and the American habit of *unseeing*.

In our contemporary moment—balanced on the cusp of a full-blown military assault on immigrants, in the midst of an ever more debilitating opioid crisis—the impulse to unsee the connections between the past and the present, health care and fentanyl, primacy and the border, could not be more tempting. Every day, we are pulled toward the black hole singularity of American exceptionalism. Every mainstream narrative about American politics—Democratic and Republican, liberal and reactionary—reaffirms this Manichaean universe without connections where cause and effect run in a single direction. The opioid epidemic flows from China and Mexico. The "crisis at the border" is *sui generis*. Students protesting the genocide in Gaza are "outside agitators." Trans and queer people—and the "woke" in general—are external threats to the white heterosexual body politic. From within this bifurcated vision, the rise of fascism in America today has nothing to do with the liberal democratic state's historical relationship to racial terror, settler and border violence, gender oppression, imperialism, and capitalist accommodation.

In this universe without connections, the nearly trillion dollars a year this country spends on its security budget, the absence of public health care, and the evisceration of social services orbit around America, never touching, never visible at the same time. Like silent, dead moons.

When I walk down the street and I see the beautiful Boy in every folded-over human being, every head down U-shape, every slumped bundle on the bus, every toe poked through every sleeping bag, every scabbed visage, I feel the pull of that singularity. When I don't hear from him for weeks at a time, and the terror shifts to that pulsing place behind my eyes, I can only think in one direction. I have authoritarian dreams. I crave blood.

But the next time I meet him for breakfast, there is a light in his eyes. He crushes me in a hug and presses my finger to the bump on his stomach where the opioid blocker is slowly dissolving under his skin into his bloodstream. I am wary—the rhythm of addiction is like this: "change talk" and failure, intention and reality, truth and lies, possibility and retreat. This could all fall apart tomorrow.

I am all too aware that my own powerlessness—like his—can tip any moment into hopelessness. And yet in this moment, here we are. We eat our breakfast. He kisses me goodbye, takes my leftovers, and walks away.

He is not of my blood. I am not of his. But we are of the connections.

ELECTION CHRONICLES

ON FIGHTING BACK
Robin D. G. Kelley

I AM baffled, as I was in 2016, as to why so many liberals are still shocked by Trump's victory—and why, in their efforts to dissect what happened, they can't get beyond their incredulity that so many people would blindly back a venal, mendacious fascist peddling racism, misogyny, xenophobia, and ableism while cloaking his anti-labor, anti-Earth, pro-corporate agenda behind a veil of white nationalism and authoritarian promises that "Trump will fix it."

We don't need to waste time trying to parse the differences between the last three elections. In all three, he won—and lost—with historic vote tallies. The message has been clear since 2016, when Trump, despite losing the popular vote to Hilary Clinton, still won the Electoral College with nearly sixty-three million votes, just three million fewer than what Obama got in 2012. Trump lost in 2020, but received seventy-four million votes—the second-largest total in U.S. history. For an incumbent presiding disastrously over the start of the COVID-19 pandemic, that astounding number of votes should have told us something. And if we were honest, we would acknowledge that Joe Biden owes most of his victory to the uprisings against police violence that momentarily shifted public opinion toward greater awareness of racial injustice and delivered Democrats an unearned historic turnout. Even though the Biden campaign aggressively distanced itself from Black Lives Matter and demands to defund the police, it benefited from the sentiment that racial injustice ought to be addressed and that liberals were best suited to address it.

Yet in all three elections, white men and women still overwhelmingly went for Trump. (Despite hopes that the overturning of *Roe* would drive a majority of white women to vote for Harris, some 53 percent of them voted for Trump, only 2 percentage points lower than in 2020.) Moreover, the much-cited demographic shift among Trump voters wasn't all that significant. True, Trump attracted more Black men this time, but about 77 percent of Black men voted for Harris, so the shocking headline, "Why did Black men vote for Trump?" is misdirected. Yes, Latino support for Trump increased, but that demographic needs to be disaggregated; it is an extremely diverse population with different political histories, national origins, and the like. And we should not be shocked that many working-class men, especially working-class men of color, did not vote for Harris. Keeanga-Yamahtta Taylor is right to point to the condescension of the Democrats for implying that sexism alone explains why a small portion of Black men and Latinos flipped toward Trump, when homelessness, hunger, rent, personal debt, and overall insecurity are on the rise. The Democrats, she explained on *Democracy Now!*, failed "to capture what is actually happening on the ground—*that* is measured not just by the historic low unemployment that Biden and Harris have talked about or by the historic low rates of poverty."

THE DEMOCRATIC PARTY lost—again—because it turned its back on working people, choosing instead to pivot to the right: recruiting Liz and Dick Cheney, quoting former Trump chief of staff John Kelly, and boasting of how many Republican endorsements Harris had rather than about her plans to lift thirty-eight million Americans out of poverty. The campaign touted the strength of the economy under Biden, but it failed to address the fact that the benefits did not seem to trickle down to large swaths of the working class. Instead, millions of workers improved their situation the old-fashioned way: through strikes and collective bargaining. The United Auto Workers, UPS workers, longshore and warehouse workers, health care workers, machinists at Boeing, baristas at Starbucks—all won significant gains. For some, Biden's public support for unions secured his place as the most pro-labor president since FDR. Perhaps, but the bar isn't that high. He campaigned on raising the federal minimum wage from $7.25 to $15, but, once taking office, quietly tabled the issue in a compromise with Republicans, choosing instead to issue an executive order raising the wage for federal contractors.

It is true that the Uncommitted movement, and the antiwar protest vote more broadly, lacked the raw numbers to change the election's outcome. But it is not an exaggeration to argue that the Biden-Harris administration's unqualified support for Israel cost the Democrats the election as much as their abandonment of the working class did. In fact, the two issues are related. The administration could have used the billions in military aid it gave to Israel for its Gaza operations during its first year alone and redirected it toward the needs of struggling working people. This figure is about a quarter of the Department of Housing and Urban Development's annual budget and 16 percent of the budget for the federal Supplemental Nutrition Assistance Program. The administration could have cut even more from the military budget, which for fiscal year 2024 stood at slightly more than $824 billion. Moreover, tens of thousands of Palestinian lives would have been spared, much of Gaza's land and infrastructure would have been spared irreversible damage, and the escalation of regional war in Lebanon and Iran would not have happened—the consequences of which remain to be seen for the federal budget.

Of course, detractors will say that the Israel lobby, especially AIPAC, would not allow it. But the Democrats' fealty to Israel is not a product of fear, nor is it simply a matter of cold electoral calculus. It is an orientation grounded in ideology. Only ideology can explain why the Biden administration did not direct UN representative Linda Thomas-Greenfield to stop providing cover for Israel's criminal slaughter and support the Security Council's resolution calling for an immediate ceasefire. And only ideology can explain why the administration and Congress did not abide by its own laws—notably the Arms Export Control Act and the Foreign Assistance Act, which prohibits the use of U.S. weapons in occupied territories and the transfer of weapons or aid to a country "which engages in a consistent pattern of gross violations of internationally recognized human rights"—and stop propping up Israel's military.

While candidate Trump had encouraged Netanyahu to "finish the job" in Gaza, President Trump, in the days leading up to his inauguration, presided over—or at least took credit for—a rapid ceasefire agreement between Israel and Hamas. (Reagan pulled a similar stunt when he secured the return of U.S. hostages from Iran on the same day he was sworn into office.) What should we make of it? The deal seems to prove Trump's campaign mantra that only he can fix it. And it will strengthen his ties with his ruling-class friends in the Gulf countries, clearing a path for the Likud Party and its rabid settler supporters to annex Gaza, in whole or in part, and continue its illegal population transfer under the guise of "reconstruction." After all, the Biden-Harris administration and the Democrats have already done all the work of "finishing the job." Gaza is virtually uninhabitable. Once we factor in disease, starvation, inadequate medical care for the wounded, and the numbers under the rubble, the actual death toll will be many times higher than the official count. And with nearly three-quarters of the casualties women and children, the U.S.-Israel alliance succeeded, long before Trump took power, in temporarily neutralizing what Israeli politicians call the Palestinian "demographic threat."

THE ELECTION indicates a rightward shift across the county. We see it in the Senate races, right-wing control of state legislatures (though here, gerrymandering played a major role), and in some of the successful state ballot measures, with the exception of abortion. But part of this shift can be explained by voter suppression, a general opposition to incumbents, and working-class disaffection expressed in low turnout. I also contend that one of the main reasons why such a large proportion of the working class voted for Trump has to do with what we old Marxists call class consciousness. Marx made a distinction between a class "in itself" and a class "for itself." The former signals status, one's relationship to means—of production, of survival, of living. The latter signals solidarity—to think like a class, to recognize that all working people, regardless of color, gender, ability, nationality, citizenship status, religion, are your comrades. When the idea of solidarity has been under relentless assault for decades, it is impossible for the class to recognize its shared interests or stand up for others with whom they may not have identical interests.

So I'm less interested in conducting a postmortem of this election and tweaking the Democrats' tactics than trying to understand how to build a movement—not in reaction to Trump, but toward workers' power, a just economy, reproductive justice, queer and trans liberation, and ending racism and patriarchy and war—in Palestine, Sudan, Congo, Haiti, and elsewhere, in our streets masquerading as a war on crime, on our borders masquerading as security, and on the earth driven by the five centuries of colonial and capitalist extraction. We have to revive the idea of solidarity, and this requires a revived class politics: not a politics that evades the racism and misogyny that pervades American life but one that confronts it directly. It is a mistake to think that white working-class support for Trump is reducible to racism and misogyny or "false consciousness" substituting for the injuries of class. As I wrote back in 2016, we cannot afford to dismiss

> the white working class's very real economic grievances. It is not a matter of disaffection *versus* racism or sexism *versus* fear. Rather, racism, class anxieties, and prevailing gender ideologies operate together, inseparably.... White working-class men understand their plight through a racial and gendered lens. For women and people of color to hold positions of privilege or power *over* them is simply unnatural and can only be explained by an act of unfairness—for example, affirmative action.

There have always been efforts to build worker solidarity, in culture and in practice. We see it in some elements of the labor movement, such as UNITE-HERE, progressive elements in SEIU, National Nurses United, Unite All Workers for Democracy, the Southern Workers Power Program, Black Workers for Justice, and Change to Win. Leading these efforts has been the tenacious but much embattled Working Families Party (WFP) and its sister organization, Working Families Power.

Their most recent survey found that growing working-class support for Trump and the MAGA Republicans does not mean working people are more conservative than wealthier Americans. Instead, it concluded, working people are "uniformly to the left of the middle and upper classes" when it comes to economic policies promoting fairness, equity, and distribution. On other issues such as immigration, education, and crime and policing, their findings are mixed and, not surprisingly, differentiated by race, gender, and political orientation. Most importantly, the WFP understands that the chief source of disaffection has been the neoliberal assault on labor and the severe weakening of workers' political and economic power.

Over the last five decades we've witnessed massive social disinvestment: the erosion of the welfare state, living-wage jobs, collective bargaining rights, union membership, government investment in education, basic democracy, and accessible and affordable housing, health care, and food. In some states, emergency financial managers have replaced elected governments, overseeing the privatization of public assets, corporate tax abatements, and cuts in employee pension funds in order to "balance" city budgets. At the same time, we have seen an exponential growth in income inequality, corporate profits, prisons, and well-funded conservative think tanks and lobbying groups whose dominance in the legislative arena has significantly weakened union rights, environmental and consumer protection, occupational safety, and the social safety net.

And the neoliberal assault is also ideological; it is an attack on the very concept of solidarity, of labor as a community with shared interests. David Harvey, Ruth Wilson Gilmore, David McNally, Nancy Fraser, Wendy Brown and many others have all compellingly articulated this challenge. In response to the 1970s strike wave and the global slump that opened the door for the neoliberal turn, the Thatcherite mantra that "there is no such thing as society; there are individual men and women" took hold. For decades unions have been disparaged as the real enemy of progress, their opponents insisting that they take dues from hardworking Americans, pay union bosses bloated salaries, kill jobs with their demand for high wages, and undermine businesses and government budgets with excessive pension packages. Remember Mitt Romney's presidential campaign talking points: workers are the "takers," capitalists are the "makers" who should decide what to pay workers. Neoliberal ideology insists that any attempt to promote equality, tolerance, and inclusion is a form of coercion over the individual and undermines freedom and choice. Such regulatory or redistributive actions, especially on the part of government, would amount to social engineering and therefore threaten liberty, competition, and natural market forces.

Generations have grown up learning that the world is a market and we are all individual entrepreneurs. Any aid or support from the state makes us dependent and unworthy. Personal responsibility and family values replace the very idea of the "social," that is to say, a nation obligated to provide for those in need. Life is governed by market principles: the idea that if we make the right investment, become more responsible for ourselves, and enhance our productivity—if we build up our human capital—we can become more competitive and, possibly, become a billionaire. Mix neoliberal logic with (white) populism and Christian nationalism and you get what Wendy Brown calls "authoritarian freedom": a freedom that posits exclusion, patriarchy, tradition, and nepotism as legitimate challenges to those dangerous, destabilizing demands of inclusion, autonomy, equal rights, secularism, and the very principle of equality. Such a toxic blend did not come out of nowhere, she insists: it was born out of the stagnation of the entire working class under neoliberal policies.

That diagnosis points toward an obvious cure. If we are going to ever defeat Trumpism, modern fascism, and wage a viable challenge to gendered racial capitalism, we must revive the old IWW slogan, "An injury to one is an injury to all." Putting that into practice means thinking beyond nation, organizing to resist mass deportation rather than vote for the party promoting it. It means seeing every racist, sexist, homophobic, and transphobic act, every brutal beating and killing of unarmed Black people by police, every denial of healthcare for the most vulnerable, as an attack on the class. It means standing up for struggling workers around the world, from Palestine to the Congo to Haiti. It means fighting for the social wage, not just higher pay and better working conditions but a reinvestment in public institutions—hospitals, housing, education, tuition-free college, libraries, parks. It means worker power and worker democracy. And if history is any guide, this cannot be accomplished through the Democratic Party alone. Trying to move the Democrats to the left hasn't worked. We need to build up independent, class-conscious, multiracial organizations such as the Working Families Party, the Poor People's Campaign, and their allies, not simply to enter the electoral arena but to effectively exercise the power to dispel ruling-class lies about how our economy and society actually work. The only way out of this mess is learning to think like a class. It's all of us or none.

ON BUYING ELECTIONS
Mark Schmitt

THE SHEER SCALE of money in politics is now hard to imagine. Over the last fifteen years, it has transformed dramatically—not just in amount, but in form, as a tiny number of wealthy individuals dominate the market for power. The thesis that the United States had become an oligarchy was mildly controversial when Martin Gilens and Benjamin Page argued it in 2014, but it is now indisputable.

According to political scientist Adam Bonica, the top 400 donors to Republican campaigns and super PACs in the 2024 election accounted for more than 60 percent of all funds spent on behalf of Republican candidates—nearly double the share from four years earlier. Meanwhile, the top 400 Democratic spenders accounted for just over a fifth of Democratic spending—much lower than the Republican share, and in line with recent historic norms, but still a staggering level of power for a very few.

All told, during the election, some $3.4 billion was spent on the two major-party candidates through reported channels. Donald

Trump's spending came mostly through "outside" groups, such as super PACs that make independent expenditures, while the majority of Kamala Harris's campaign spending moved through her campaign. After Elon Musk, head of the newly created Department of Government Efficiency, whose reportable political spending totaled nearly $280 million, the top spenders overall were Miriam Adelson, widow of casino owner Sheldon Adelson, and Timothy Mellon, grandson of banker Andrew Mellon, a sort of Musk *avant la lettre* who controlled both a massive fortune and a large swath of government as Treasury Secretary through all of the Republican administrations of the 1920s and into the Depression. Mellon was followed by Richard and Elizabeth Uihlein, owners of a packaging company and major funders of groups involved in 2020 election denial. The top seven spenders all supported Republicans exclusively, and six put in nine-figure sums. It's notable that, with the partial exception of Musk, none are executives of publicly traded or public-facing corporations, suggesting a shift in power within contemporary capitalism.

There's routine popular outrage at this state of affairs, but remarkably little political will to do anything about it. It wasn't always this way. A generation ago, the idea of improving American democracy was all but synonymous with the effort to reduce the influence of money and wealth on elections. Bipartisan initiatives to limit "soft money" contributions (donations made to political parties) at the federal level, and to implement public financing of campaigns at the state and local level, were central to the agendas of John McCain and Russ Feingold as much as they were to old-line organizations such as Common Cause, the original "good-government" organization, founded in 1970 by a Republican.

Today, though, the issue hardly registers among elected officials; few other than the diligent Sheldon Whitehouse, Democratic senator from Rhode Island, pay it more than lip service. The bipartisan coalitions that once drove valuable reforms are long gone. The momentum behind comprehensive pro-democracy legislation, including public financing for congressional elections, fizzled out in the first half of the Biden administration. The Federal Election Commission (FEC), the agency charged with enforcing what remains of federal law, has been effectively defunct for at least a decade because of obstruction by Republican appointees. And although voters in Maine enacted a limit on contributions to super PACs in 2024, few other states have done much to limit political spending or to expand public financing.

One reason the cause has faded from view is that so many competing democratic priorities have crowded onto the agenda, from partisan redistricting and voter suppression to election denialism and genuine threats of authoritarian rule and kleptocracy. The docket is packed. Opportunities for progress at the federal level and through federal courts are few.

And earlier, with the emergence of a base of small donors across both parties—particularly the three million individual donors to Barack Obama's 2008 campaign—Democrats and many reformers became complacent that the enthusiastic masses could fund campaigns without the ethical corner-cutting of the Clinton years, when the president was directly involved in raising soft money (something that, in the Trump era, seems as trivial as jaywalking). An optimistic 2010 report by four political scientists, "Reform in an Age of Networked Campaigns," argued that the emergence of small donors, combined with reforms to introduce public financing, could create a kind of virtuous cycle to offset the political influence of the wealthy. A few campaigns since, such as Bernie Sanders's two presidential efforts, have reflected this commitment—albeit without the public financing part—but for the most part, the optimism of that moment has faded. Most Democrats and Republicans fell back into the pattern of seeking support from wealthy donors and outside groups.

It is tempting to see the Supreme Court's *Citizens United* ruling as the turning point in the concentration of the market for political influence—and in terms of timing and the anything-goes message the Court sent, it is. More legally significant, though, were the *SpeechNOW* decision by the D.C. circuit court of appeals, also in 2010, which allowed the creation of super PACs that only make independent expenditures in support of campaigns, and the wholly contrived IRS scandal of 2011, in which Representative Jim Jordan alleged that the tax agency had unfairly scrutinized right-wing nonprofits. That baseless investigation in turn forced the IRS to declare that such nonprofits, known as social welfare organizations, could spend up to half of their budgets on election-related activities. These tax-exempt nonprofits have become a mainstay of "dark money" funding.

But we should resist being nostalgic about the problems and solutions of the 1990s—and about the 2002 law, the McCain-Feingold Act, that the Court partly overturned with *Citizens United*. As much as we might want to, we can't go back to that moment. Instead, we need a new way of thinking about the pervasive influence of money and inequality on democracy. True, the issue is now in abeyance—there are few near-term opportunities for change, and it may seem like nothing's happening—but it's in such times as these that advocates can develop new ideas, strategies, and coalitions for the moment when circumstances change.

CONTRARY TO popular perception, McCain-Feingold was not primarily about whether money is speech, whether corporations possess free speech rights, or whether corporations are people. (Regulations on money used to disseminate speech are a form of constraint on speech, and corporations do have First Amendment rights, though not necessarily on the same terms as individuals.) Instead, it sought to define the boundaries of an election: What kind of spending should be treated as if it were a contribution to an election campaign, subject to the contribution limits of the Federal Election Campaign Act and a much older ban on corporate contributions?

In effect, campaign finance regulations define a narrow exception to First Amendment rights. Within the boundaries of an election, speech can be limited in the interest of reducing corruption—much like laws that limit electioneering within seventy-five feet of a voting place. But outside the campaign, broader First Amendment rights apply. Reacting to a 1990s messaging tactic—broadcast ads close to Election Day evading regulation by naming an opposing candidate in a disingenuous call to action like "Call Congressman Jones and ask why he always raises taxes," but not using phrases like "vote against

Jones"—Congress specified a criterion for determining whether speech fell within the boundary of an election. If such speech named a candidate at all, it was subject to regulation.

When a right-wing organization called Citizens United put out a pay-per-view documentary called *Hillary: The Movie* during the 2008 presidential primaries, the FEC thus ruled that it should be considered a campaign expense, subject to limits. Citizens United challenged the ruling, and the Supreme Court rejected the FEC's decision, finding that communications like the documentary, or ads for it—without coordination with a campaign—fell outside the limits on campaign contributions.

But as partisan and issue polarization has deepened over the last quarter century, the boundary defined by naming a candidate has faded in importance. An ad, mailer, or other communication that doesn't mention a candidate or party at all—one that solely focuses on an issue—can have as much influence on voters as one that does. And money spent on such communications, along with nudges to social media, traditional media, and the world of niche podcasts, can shape the issue environment to a profound degree.

Indeed, during the 2024 election, one of Musk's interventions through his America PAC was to circulate a petition asking voters to pledge to support the First and Second Amendments, along with a sweepstakes offering a million dollars to a few signers. The sweepstakes may have been illegal under Pennsylvania law, but the petition itself was an effective way of identifying and targeting Trump supporters—seeding the message that Democrats threaten both those rights without mentioning the election or candidates. Even if the wink-and-nod intent is to influence the election, such a petition, and the money used to circulate it, would certainly fall within the protections of the First Amendment under any interpretation—and should. Other spending to gain political influence—such as the hundreds of millions of dollars flowing through the Federalist Society and related entities to recruit, promote, and influence federal judges and Supreme Court justices—also doesn't fall anywhere near the boundaries of an election.

The older reform agenda was based on a model of the role of money in politics in which candidates, and to a lesser degree political parties, were the primary actors. The idea was that candidates need funds to communicate with voters (until recently, by way of costly radio and television ads) and turn to donors—who might be ideological allies, friends or professional acquaintances of the candidate, or parties with an interest in some government decision—for those funds. Desperate for resources, candidates would invite corruption as they solicited these funds, or they would build channels such as soft money to evade legal limits. Either way, the result was an objectionable dependence on donors—what Harvard legal scholar Lawrence Lessig called "dependence corruption"—even in the absence of provable quid pro quo influence on official decisions.

Given this picture of the problem, reformers sought to limit the influence of donors on candidates and elected officials, either through individual contribution limits (the Court in 1974 had ruled limits on total spending unconstitutional), or through some form of public financing that would reduce dependence, such as matching small contributions, providing a fixed grant of funds, or giving every citizen a voucher to donate to the candidates or campaigns of their choice. But as candidates and operatives found new ways to evade the limits, the futility of relying on those limits alone became evident. After that, small-donor public financing came to seem like the only viable solution.

Today, it may no longer be true that candidates are the main actors in campaign finance. The current oligarchy is one in which spenders move and control large pools of political money on their own, attaching themselves to candidates or causes like the mercenary armies of the Middle Ages. There is a reason I use the term "spenders" rather than "donors." Billionaires are not simply handing money over to politicians and campaigns; they are running their own political operations.

Some are individuals with sophisticated political staff, deploying mostly their own money: the likes of Musk and Ken Griffin for Republicans, Michael Bloomberg and Reid Hoffman for Democrats. Others are super PAC entrepreneurs—pooling money, gaining significant wealth in their own right, and showing little loyalty to candidates. The organizers of one massive super PAC supporting Florida governor Ron DeSantis in the 2024 Republican primaries moved smoothly over to Trump later in the year. Despite FEC regulations prohibiting coordination between super PACs and campaigns, money can keep flowing through freestanding entities with none of the accountability to voters that parties, candidates, and elected officials (in theory) have.

WHAT IS to be done? A reform agenda designed to address this new form of oligarchy could make some incremental improvements. Public financing should be at the heart of it, to give candidates a way to go more directly to voters. New York City's small-donor matching system is still probably the best model. Coupled with ranked-choice voting in the primaries, it created a competitive race for mayor in 2021, and it will likely do so again this year (though Mayor Eric Adams's indictment shows that such a generous system is vulnerable to abuses of its own). Reforms should also try to move money back into political parties, which, unlike the super PACs and their operators, have long-term interests and can be held accountable. (Minnesota's small-donor program, which provides an instant tax refund for donations up to $75 to both candidates and parties, is a promising model.) And while the FEC may never be able to reclaim its regulatory role as currently structured, the IRS—in a future administration, of course, since Trump's certainly won't pursue this—should restore the principle that election-related activities should be no more than incidental to the work of any tax-exempt nonprofit.

But with such concentrated wealth, and with the market for political power in the hands of a few, there's only so much that can be done in the traditional domain of campaign finance law while still respecting the right to free expression. The problem is no longer "money in politics"; it's just money. Anything we can do to break its concentration—through taxation, antitrust enforcement, and public ownership of public goods—will help reduce the political power it commands.

ON REBUILDING LABOR
Janice Fine & Benjamin Schlesinger

IN SEPTEMBER 2023, Joe Biden became the first sitting president to walk a picket line when he joined striking United Auto Workers in Wayne County, Michigan. A decade earlier, under the Obama administration, Democrats had asked the union to make concessions in bargaining to save the auto industry—and it did, accepting cuts to wages, pensions, and retiree health care along with a two-tier wage system that hired newcomers at a much lower wage. Now, Biden was paying them back, supporting their demands for a larger piece of the pie, and the UAW's "Stand Up Strike" succeeded in reversing the givebacks of the recession.

In the most pro-labor White House and Congress in eighty years, Biden pulled nearly every lever of state power to strengthen existing unions. His appointments—Jennifer Abruzzo as general counsel of the National Labor Relations Board (NLRB), Lina Khan as chair of the Federal Trade Commission (FTC), and Julie Su as acting secretary of the Department of Labor (DOL)—secured historic gains for worker power and economic justice. And the administration passed part of an ambitious industrial policy that created thousands of union jobs in energy, construction, and the auto industry, with its most visible accomplishments—new manufacturing facilities making microchips and state-of-the-art electric vehicles—forming a major part of Kamala Harris's campaign pitch to working-class voters. But on Election Day, Trump garnered the majority of votes from those earning under $100,000—a class dealignment compared with Biden's victory in 2020.

In the blame game that followed Harris's loss, union leadership has been clear: you can't put this on us. They are only partly right. According to both public exit polling and internal union surveys, the labor movement came through—a large majority of union members voted for Harris. While some polls had Biden tied with Trump among union members before he dropped out, early returns in some battleground states showed a commanding twenty-point margin for Harris. In every swing state, UNITE HERE and the AFL-CIO's field program made personal contact with millions of their members. Organizers persuaded tens of thousands of voters to side with their economic interests and reward the administration that had done so much for them with another term. This spadework is what labor has traditionally been good at. It's entirely possible that unions' internal organizing efforts saved Senate seats in Nevada, Wisconsin, and Michigan along with overperforming in down-ballot legislative races in Pennsylvania.

The Biden administration saw in unions what unions would like to see in themselves: a broad and powerful organization of the working class that could reshape American society and partner with them to end the neoliberal era. The problem with that vision is that it isn't true. When only 6 percent of private-sector workers belong to unions, unions are no longer a legitimate stand-in for the working class. Most working-class Americans have no experience with unions in their daily lives. If they did, it would make a difference in how they see the world. Unions have historically been schools of democracy for their members. What has always set them apart from volunteer organizations is that unions don't choose their members—meaning that they need to engage disparate groups of workers in ways that build solidarity across difference. As the old saying goes, class is knowing which side of the fence you are on; class consciousness is knowing who is there with you. When unions were strong and growing, Democratic campaign efforts were buoyed by pro-union messaging and turnout operations that meant something to much of the American public. Today, far from ennobling a candidate in the minds of all working Americans, a union's presidential endorsement can at best hope to shore up the vote from workers lucky enough to count themselves in a union's ranks.

When Biden spoke about growing up in Scranton, Pennsylvania, and the kitchen-table wisdom of his father; when he repeated the truism that "the middle class built America, and unions built the middle class"—he was talking to an almost insignificant segment of voters. No amount of infrastructure investment for union jobs could convince most workers that the bell was tolling for them—especially not when their wages were stagnating and their cost of living was skyrocketing. The images of Democrats in union halls simply did not project the idea of support for the larger working class the party wanted it to—they only spotlighted unions as a club that the vast majority of workers could only dream of joining. On November 5, most workers turned out for the candidate they felt would tackle inflation and cater to their immediate needs as consumers, not the one promising to protect an abstract right to organize. Of course, Trump's promise of mass deportations, paired with his administration's likely gutting of labor standards, will bring only misery. The fastest-growing sectors in the U.S. economy will continue to rely on low wages and workplace tyranny, only to be cheered on by a president who bragged about violating overtime the same way he bragged about violating women.

BUT THAT DOESN'T mean the end of labor. In fact, rebuilding the labor movement and a political party dedicated to fighting for the entire working class may well be the only strategy for defeating Trumpism and delivering a more just society.

Where do we start? Throwing everything we've got at organizing the unorganized and revitalizing the political education of existing members, re-polarizing American politics around social class instead of insisting on a tent big enough for Bernie Sanders and Mark Cuban to fit at either end. We need a party that welcomes the hatred of the economic royalists—not just the Elon Musks of the world but the faceless pharma CEOs who are profiting off of the desperation of the sick and elderly and the hedge fund executives who continue to ship jobs overseas, privatize public services, and drive up the cost of housing. The current version of the party might have successfully defeated Trump once, but it will never change the material conditions that made his rise possible.

True, the odds are stacked against us. Given the Republican trifecta in Washington, we will certainly not be able to pass labor law reform that removes formidable barriers to organizing anytime soon, and the leadership of the NLRB, DOL, and FTC will no longer be our comrades in arms. On the contrary, as Trump did in 2016, we can expect appointees who will make millions no longer eligible for overtime, remove protections from excessive heat exposure, and weaken liability for wage theft. Employers, emboldened by an administration firmly on their side, will still fight organizing drives tooth and nail, with consequences for union-busting coming too little and too late. Workers in care, hospitality, retail, gig work, and even manufacturing remain spread out across many small workplaces. The proliferation of temp agencies, the misclassification of workers as independent contractors rather than employees, and layers of subcontracting between corporations and their workforce will continue to bedevil organizing.

But this is not the whole story. The call is also coming from inside the house. Most unions simply aren't investing significantly in organizing of any kind. Even when presented with workers who want to join—by worker centers, for example, or by the nascent Emergency Worker Organizing Committee—many unions flatly decline to take them in, citing old arguments against "hot shop organizing," the idea that unions should accept workplaces regardless of whether they represent a significant number of workers in the sector. Unions reason that without density, they won't be able to deliver significant gains, and individual workplaces will cost too much to represent. But in a world where unionization rates in many industries are already below 5 percent, caution is no longer tenable. We can't afford to turn down any of the 52 percent of non-union workers who say that, given the opportunity, they would vote to join a union today. Part of this effort will require unions to radically rethink their organizing strategy and invest in distributed models focused on supporting organizers within a given workplace rather than relying on paid staff.

For decades, many unions have insisted that the hundreds of worker centers and other "alt labor" groups—which have organized the likes of taxi drivers and domestic, carwash, construction, nail salon, warehouse, food manufacturing, farm, and nursery workers—would be flimsy and fleeting. But many are still thriving, intensively organizing specific industries and interested in partnering with unions. And since so many of these groups' members are undocumented workers, they will be on the frontlines of fighting Trump's deportation machine. In anticipation of those mass deportations, worker centers like Arriba Las Vegas, Arise Chicago, and Centro Comunitario de Trabajadores in New Bedford are helping workers who are organizing and bringing workplace violation cases to file for deferred enforcement of immigration cases. They, too, are the labor movement.

Organizing at scale and pioneering new models is difficult and risky—and will certainly be expensive. But it is critical. Sectoral bargaining alone, without workers organizing, won't build a fighting working class: *fighting* builds a fighting working class. When the worker-to-worker organizing at Starbucks first began, most union strategists said that it was a fool's errand; they would never get to a first contract. Some 521 shops and 11,947 workers later, Starbucks is bargaining. The Union of Southern Service Workers is energetically organizing Dollar General and Waffle House workers. Winning takes a willingness to try several times, as the UAW demonstrated when it succeeded at unionizing a Volkswagen plant in Chattanooga this past April after failed votes in 2014 and 2019.

We don't have another four years of pro-union policy. What we do have are existing unions with substantial treasuries—some $35 billion in total, according to research by Chris Bohner—and a workforce with significant grievances. We need to bring them together. Unions need to invest in worker-to-worker organizing and convince millions more workers that voting for Trump won't fix their economic problems—voting to form a union will.

ON THE IMPERIAL BOOMERANG
Noura Erakat

IN THE FALLOUT of the election, a stream of social media content—some from passionate Harris supporters, some from lesser-evil Democratic voters, and some, presumably, from people simply lashing out, horrified and distraught at Trump's win—took to blaming Palestinians for the outcome.

My initial fury at these statements eventually gave way to analysis. How could so many people be so callous and so wrong? The tendency to scapegoat in moments of crisis, along with pervasive anti-Palestinian racism, are surely factors, but there are larger forces at work as well. Many had seen Palestinians protesting the Democratic Party, but thanks to widespread censorship and media bias, most of them also almost certainly had not seen the stream of atrocities in Gaza that had been taking place for over a year: five-year-old Hind Rajab begging for someone to save her; the body of Sidra Hassouna split in two and hanging on a beam of a destroyed building; Sha'ban al-Dalou burned to death while attached to an IV drip in a hospital; a civilian crew in Gaza tearing through heavy stones with their bare hands to reach a young girl, wearing white tennis shoes and a green sweatsuit that her parents must have been proud to dress her in, trapped under the rubble of a bombed-out building for fifteen hours, only for her to die before they reach her.

But beyond a lack of awareness of the vast devastation, many Americans also haven't heard what it has to do with the United States, and with the Democratic Party in particular: the fact that, in the year following October 7, the Biden administration sent nearly $23 billion to Israel with no red lines; that it vetoed four UN Security Council resolutions demanding a ceasefire; that Secretary of State Antony Blinken ignored the U.S. government's own determination that Israel was blocking humanitarian aid to Gaza when he delivered a statement under oath to Congress last May; that the United States has violated its own laws—including the Arms Export Control Act, Section 620i of the Foreign Assistance Act, and National Security Memorandum-20—conditioning U.S. military aid to state belligerents on their compliance with U.S. and international laws of war; that the United States has undermined the authority of both the International Court of Justice (ICJ) and the International Criminal Court (ICC); and that 107 members of Congress sent a letter to the United Nations two weeks before the election threatening to withdraw U.S. funding and support for the organization if it allowed its members to unseat Israel, as the General Assembly had done with the South African apartheid regime in 1974.

Simply put, most people have no idea to what extent this genocide is being perpetrated not only by Israel but also by the United States. For a solid majority of the center-left, what is happening in Gaza is tragic but ultimately less important than the most significant existential threat: the ascendance of Trump. During the run-up to the election, the argument goes, we Palestinian and Arab Americans should have understood that resisting fascism in the United States is the primary goal and gotten in line accordingly.

But resisting fascism *is* our collective goal. We just know that in order to resist it, we have to fight it on two fronts of U.S. state violence: at home and abroad. Because if the United States, together with Israel, manages to disembowel the ICJ, the ICC, the UN, and a broader global order built after the Holocaust and World War II, no one is safe. The fact that Israel has committed genocide, turned humans into walking bombs in its pager attack in Lebanon, and decimated countries while the UN Security Council watches passively should concern all of us. As Colombian President Gustavo Petro warned back in December 2023, "What we are seeing in Gaza is a rehearsal of the future."

If only more people in the United States had taken his words seriously. During the election, the work of several initiatives, such as the Uncommitted movement and Not Another Bomb, emphasized the centrality of ending U.S. warmaking to a progressive agenda. Other efforts, like Abandon Biden/Harris, went further, highlighting the similarity between right-wing fascism and "authoritarian liberalism." All labored to make the entwinement of domestic and foreign policy visible—but that message was drowned out by the dehumanization of Palestinians, itself underwritten by the War on Terror's racialization of Arabs and Muslims as presumptively guilty terrorists.

It was thus unsurprising that throughout the election cycle, nearly all the mainstream liberal pundits sounding the alarm about white supremacy, jingoism, xenophobia, and political violence failed to connect these things to U.S. imperial violence. What if, rather than blaming Palestinians, Arab Americans, and American Muslims, these pundits had seen their treatment—under Biden and for decades before him—as central to the Trump-led repression looming before us?

IN HIS searing 1950 polemic *Discourse on Colonialism,* Martinican writer Aimé Césaire wrote of the "boomerang effect," whereby violence in the colonial periphery manifests itself in the colonial metropole. Hitler's genocide of European Jews, he noted, was modeled after European rule over African and Asian colonies. (He may have had in mind the German extermination of the Nama and Herero people in Namibia during their period of colonial rule from 1884 and 1915—a period of brutality that scarcely registered in Europe while it was taking place.) Some seventy-five years later, Césaire's point has been borne out many times over: there is no clear dividing line between a colonial power's imperial geography and its metropole.

In the early twentieth century, when the U.S. army in the Philippines reoriented itself to address counterinsurgency and cement colonial rule over its newly conquered territories and peoples, law enforcement at home transformed itself in its image. Drawing on the new military model, police reformers revamped their departments to feature professional academies, mounted police units, surveillance, racial profiling, anticipatory policing, mapping, and weapons training. Counterinsurgency in Vietnam further militarized U.S. police, ushering SWAT teams, military-grade weapons, and a willingness to deploy disproportionate force into urban policing. At the turn of the century, the so-called War on Terror expanded presidential authority, severely curtailed civil rights, and made a mockery of the Constitution just as quickly as it did international law.

Today we are living out the latest chapter of this story, and this time the boomerang has come hurtling back with astonishing speed. Already, the genocide has expanded authoritarianism—its U.S. architects ignoring the 84 percent of Democrats who supported a ceasefire, censoring the media, and suppressing academic freedom—as well as increased police power, with snipers on university rooftops training their weapons at unarmed protesters a frequent occurrence.

This might have been a galvanizing moment. The entwinement between state and military violence could have made more vivid how Islamophobic and anti-Palestinian racism in the United States fuels endless war abroad, and how, in turn, this endless war continues to villainize Palestinians, Arabs, and Muslims. But for most, that moment of recognition has not come. Instead, abuse against Palestinians has been normalized, and harmful precedents have been established that make other vulnerable communities less safe as well.

CONSIDER THE repression that Palestinians and their allies have endured in the United States over the last year. Palestine Legal reports that in the five months after October 7, the organization received over 1,500 reports of harassment, abuse, doxing, and loss of employment—a seven-fold increase over the whole of 2020. The Council on American-Islamic Relations likewise reports that in the final quarter of 2023, it received a 178 percent increase in reports compared to the same period in 2022. And all this is to say nothing of outright violence against Palestinians, including the shooting of three Palestinian American college students in Burlington, Vermont, who were targeted for wearing keffiyehs and speaking Arabic (and which left twenty-year-old Brown University student Hisham Awartani paralyzed), and the killing of six-year-old Wadea Al-Fayoume, who was stabbed twenty-six times in his home by his seventy-one-year-old landlord.

While these crimes were not state sponsored, they are the direct fallout of the U.S. government's complicity in ongoing genocide and its decades-old anti-terrorism laws, which, as Darryl Li has highlighted, have been constructed specifically to target Palestinians. From the first mention of terrorism in a federal statute in 1969 to the introduction of a government terrorism blacklist and the first immigration law to include terrorism as grounds for exclusion and deportation, all of these efforts historically targeted Palestinians and the Palestinian struggle for liberation more generally.

In 2001, the Bush administration shut down the Holy Land Foundation (HLF), a humanitarian organization that built orphanages, distributed food, supported schools, and provided health care to Palestinians under Israeli rule, as well as in refugee camps. The administration charged its founders with working "on behalf of Hamas" under the Patriot Act, despite the fact that the recipients of the Foundation's grants, such as municipal Zakat committees in Hebron, Tulkarm, and Nablus had also received U.S. government aid. During the spurious 2008 trial, an anonymous witness—who turned out to be an Israeli intelligence officer—used "secret evidence" on the stand for the first time in a U.S. criminal court, a clear violation of the Sixth Amendment. He knew the HLF had terror affiliations, he argued on the stand, because he could "smell Hamas" on them—which was enough to sentence the five cofounders of the Foundation to between fifteen and sixty-five years in prison.

Once established, however, these repressive measures have had impacts far beyond Palestinians. By March 2023, Georgia police had arrested and charged forty-two activists protesting the expansion of Cop City, a $90 million militarized police training facility that requires the clear-cutting of Atlanta's largest clear space, charging them with domestic terrorism. Six months later, Georgia's attorney general charged five of the activists with terrorism and three of the bail fund organizers with money laundering—expanding the list of targets to include those providing the protesters legal and financial support. And in May 2024, the state legislature in

Tennessee adopted HB 2348/SB 2610, which allowed the state to target other social movements with terrorism charges—primarily environmental ones, as well as those who, like Black Lives Matter, declare their solidarity with Palestinians.

In similar fashion, attacks on free speech that target Palestinians empower the right-wing agenda against discourses and programs on racial justice. In the fall of 2023, Elise Stefanik became the supposed champion against antisemitism during congressional hearings that grilled university presidents for failing to do enough to end what she called the threat of genocide of Jews by students who were protesting an actual genocide of Palestinians. Ultimately, the hearings compelled two presidents to resign, their feverish attempts to repress and punish students ultimately falling short of Stefanik's mark.

When students took it upon themselves to pressure their institutions to divest from weapons manufacturers and other industries sustaining this violence—which includes scholasticide, the killing of teachers and students and the destruction of educational infrastructure—some university presidents called on police to brutalize their students while others, like the president of UCLA, allowed outside mobs to violently attack students while the police watched. A year later, universities have hired private security firms to repress their student protests and to limit speech so much on campus as to be tantamount to theater, with free speech as the right to be heard, but not to challenge power. So far, three tenured faculty—all American citizens—have been fired or put on leave for criticizing Israel: Maura Finkelstein, Steven

Thrasher, and Jodi Dean. These harsh punishments normalized the University of Illinois Urbana-Champaign's precedent-setting revocation of a tenure offer to Palestinian professor Steven Salaita in 2014 for his tweets criticizing Israel during its fifty-one-day onslaught of Gaza.

In January, Columbia Law Professor Katherine Franke resigned after twenty-five years of an illustrious academic career because of institutional harassment and scrutiny she endured for pointing out—correctly—that Israeli students who complete their military service and come to Columbia have "been known to harass Palestinians and other students" on campus. Most recently, NYU established that Zionism, a political ideology, is a protected class within the meaning of Title VI of the 1964 Civil Rights Act—further restricting political agency and speech. Nine universities have suspended their chapters of Students for Justice in Palestine; in Florida, Governor Ron DeSantis has tried to ban the group altogether.

ALL OF THIS has cleared a neat path for the second Trump administration, which will be all too happy to intensify the securitization of Palestinians and the Palestinian liberation struggle for the sake of expanding police power and government repression. Even while taking credit for the ceasefire in Gaza, Trump's national security advisor, Michael Waltz, expressed alignment with the Biden administration's murderous Middle East policy, described the pager attack in Lebanon as movie-worthy, and framed the college protests—which Biden had condemned at every turn—as wind under Hamas's sails:

> Every time [Hamas] got the news of these antisemitic protests on our college campuses, and that Hezbollah could be coming in, and seeing calls for regime change against the democratically elected Israeli government, they thought they were winning and could continue to sacrifice their own people to turn world opinion against the Israelis.

Congress already seems to be in lockstep with this new trajectory. Weeks after Trump's election win, a majority of the House—including fifteen Democrats—approved HR 9495, an amendment that would give Congress the authority to revoke the tax-exempt status of any nonprofit organization it accuses of having terrorist affinities, without access to the evidence or the right to due process. Robust support for the bill is predicated on its stated purpose of targeting Palestine-related activity, yet if it is adopted by the Senate, it will be used to quash broad swaths of civil society—particularly those in opposition to Trump. The bill's ally outside of government is Project Esther, a Heritage Foundation initiative that seeks to combat antisemitism by targeting groups it identifies as part of a "Hamas Support Network," including organizations like Jewish Voice for Peace and Students for Justice in Palestine. The initiative manifests the International Holocaust Remembrance Alliance's definition of antisemitism, which includes protest of Israel and Israeli policy, at its full and most dangerous potential.

By now, it should be clear that conservative agendas continue to use Palestine as a Trojan horse. Yet the liberal establishment has not raised the alarms. Worse, they have often served as the right's complicit partner, oblivious to the precedents that Trump is now inheriting: broader police power, unaccountable presidential power, generalized repression, and gross restrictions on speech. The vicious culture of anti-Palestinian racism they have helped normalize strengthens Trump's insidious narrative of migrants as terrorist threats, all as part of a massive push to facilitate deportations, ramp up surveillance, and further militarize the border. Among the flurry of executive orders he signed on Inauguration Day is one promising to deport foreign nationals who "provide aid, advocacy, or support for foreign terrorists." Just two days later, a pro-Israel group submitted a list of 100 students and 20 faculty with visas in the United States to the Trump administration urging their deportation. The administration then issued another executive order encouraging faculty, students, and administrators to surveil one another and report students who participate in pro-Palestinian protest, threatening to deport protesters who are in the United States on a visa. Meanwhile, a New York–based national defense and cyber intelligence company, Stellar Technologies, pledged to use its AI technology to help identify masked protesters—an effort it calls "Operation Wrath of Zion."

For all these reasons, Trump's second coming can't be understood without turning our gaze outward, toward a broader geography of U.S. state violence. In November 2023, in between rounds of U.S.-made bombs raining down on Al Shifa Hospital, Palestinian children in Gaza organized a press conference in front of the hospital, entreating us to do what we can to save them: "We come now to shout and invite you to protect us; we want to live, we want peace. . . . we want to live as the other children live." Under what conditions did children have to organize a press conference asking us not to let them be slaughtered? And should we be surprised that, after such gruesome crimes have been committed in our name, fascism has found fertile ground here at home? For fifteen months, Palestinians and their allies protested relentlessly and, at times, heroically, not only to stop a genocide but to salvage and preserve core humanitarian principles governing life within the United States, insisting that genocide is suicide. Surviving this next chapter demands that we see ourselves as the rest of the world sees us too.

ON A REAL POST-NEOLIBERAL AGENDA
Marshall Steinbaum

THE YEAR 2014 was a heady moment in the economic policy world. That spring, French economist Thomas Piketty's *Capital in the Twenty-First Century* was published in English to astounding commercial and intellectual success. The book painted a devastating picture of the post–Cold War economic order, uniting groundbreaking empirical evidence with a comprehensive theory explaining the vast accumulation of wealth and power at the top of the global economic pyramid. And it appeared at a moment when the apparatus of the Democratic Party needed just such a shock.

Recovery from the 2008 financial crisis, itself a consequence of Clinton-era financial deregulation, had been too long and too weak in the making; inequality ratcheted ever upward and jobs continued disappearing overseas. These trends signaled that the policies, rhetoric, and personnel of the Obama administration simply weren't up to the task. Piketty's reception, though not without pushback, helped cement consensus that something had to be done, kicking off a spirited effort within the progressive policy world to reform the Democrats' approach to the economy.

Now that Trump has dealt a decisive deathblow to the post-Obama political system, it's worth taking stock of where that moment went. Postmortems on Bidenomics have tended to focus on climate provisions, rising protectionism in trade, and the macroeconomics of stimulus and inflation. The limits of the administration's "industrial policy," touted as marking a "post-neoliberal" paradigm shift, have been extensively documented; it was always a national security program first—an ill-conceived reaction to fears of a rising China—and a pro-worker agenda second, if at all. The bigger, less talked-about picture is the long arc of ten years of failure to confront inequality after the Piketty moment in 2014. Across four key policy areas—taxation, labor standards, the welfare state, and antitrust—Democrats could have pursued a comprehensive program for combating plutocracy and empowering workers. But the opportunity was frittered away through a relentless focus on playing by the old rules of policy debate and routing reform through the usual elite channels, insulated from—and often outright hostile to—the voices and views of on-the-ground constituencies. All that came at the cost of forging a durable political coalition.

The result is that Trump is now festooning his second administration with the wealthiest people in world history. Getting out of this mess requires clarity about what happened over the last decade that led to this dire situation: exactly how Piketty's clarion message was absorbed into, and then quietly killed by, a political system that sorely needed to take it to heart to have any hope of defending itself.

PROGRESSIVE TAXATION is the single most important policy lever for reducing the power of the rich—not because it raises revenue that can be redistributed via public programs or directly to the poor, but because it imposes a de facto statutory maximum on income or wealth, eliminating the incentive to hoard the economy's resources. Unrestrained capital accumulation is the main reason for economic stagnation and the hollowing out of productive capacity. Conversely, as Piketty's research shows, economic growth is both faster and more equitably distributed—meaning *pre*-tax top income shares are low—in jurisdictions where effective tax rates at the top are highest. When elites face limits on how much they can take home, they use their dominant position to grab less, so there's more for everyone else.

Treating progressive taxation as a political rather than a fiscal phenomenon has two key advantages. First, it avoids playing into the hands of austerity politics, as Democratic talk about taxes always has. The point is not for the government to "raise money" to pay for programs or balance the federal budget; in fact, since the aim is to destroy the tax base north of the threshold for the top bracket, the less money steep progressive taxation raises, the more effective the policy. And second, talking this way focuses attention on class war: the reason you're poor is that they're rich. The political logic is self-sustaining. Straight talk about combating plutocracy grows broad-based working-class support, which makes it possible to sustain serious progressive taxation over time, which in turn wins more people to the constituency. Bernie Sanders's attacks on "millionaires and billionaires," AOC's onetime slogan that "every billionaire is a policy failure": their movement-building success with that message, even in the face of mainstream Democrats' hostility toward it, speaks for itself. So does Claudia Sheinbaum's recent victory in Mexico, which rode on the motto, "For the good of all, the poor first."

All of this was more or less the explicit message of *Capital in the Twenty-First Century*, especially as it pertained to progressive taxation. But that message could not break through the hard shell of Democratic common sense about fiscal policy, which is structured around two entrenched strands: a right-wing strand that prioritizes fiscal rectitude, and a liberal strand that views taxes, particularly progressive taxes, primarily as a way to answer the perennial objection "How are you going to pay for it?"

When Senate Democrats were strategizing how to oppose the Tax Cuts and Jobs Act during Trump's first term, for example, they decided that highlighting its fiscal irresponsibility, through citations of Congressional Budget Office scores, was the only way to peel off Republican votes or mount an opposition campaign. A senator told me exactly that when I briefed the Senate Democratic Caucus on how to message on progressive tax policy. But the fight on the floor of Congress is not the only fight that matters. Although Democrats all voted against the bill, they succeeded in peeling away only *one* Republican vote; the legislation passed anyway. In other words, Democrats not only failed to block the bill using this approach; they failed to use the moment to break from the old technocratic rules of policy discussion, politicize the way we assess tax policy, and build popular consensus and pressure outside of Washington.

There are reasons Democrats find it hard to embrace this talk, of course. One is that the party itself has plenty of plutocrats in its ranks.

Another, less well appreciated, is that Democratic Party–aligned policy experts and advisors strenuously seek to preserve their credibility in backroom political convenings, which are primarily composed of well-credentialed people affiliated with both parties—and not, that is, with voices from or accountable to popular constituencies, who speak the passionate language of anti-plutocracy. Adding a giant dose of class war to tax policy certainly would have upset that tradition, but there was nothing but political will standing in the way of Democratic leaders insisting it be done, whatever the consequences for the professional prestige of their most senior staffers.

Insofar as the progressive tax policy championed by Piketty had any presence in the Biden administration, it was on two fronts: enhancing the enforcement budget of the Internal Revenue Service and enacting an international minimum corporate profit tax rate. But both of these efforts fell far short of the bold vision Piketty elaborated. The first even reflected Larry Summers's critique of Piketty: Why should we raise marginal tax rates on the rich to 90 percent, he complained, when we're not fully enforcing liability at 40 percent? And the second got mired in the intractable morass of international negotiations; it was eventually enacted abroad but not in the United States due to a total blockade in Congress.

WHEN IT COMES to labor standards, Biden has been feted as the most pro-labor president since FDR—at least by political commentators and union leaders, if by not the rank and file. His appointments to the National Labor Relations Board (NLRB) were an improvement over the status quo, though they have now been undone by Trump. But when it comes to moving legislation that would outlast appointees, the Biden administration was no different from its Democratic predecessors.

In 2021, the Protecting the Right to Organize (PRO) Act was introduced by Democratic labor committee leaders in both houses of Congress, representing the agreed-upon asks of the labor movement's legislative affairs advisors: heightened penalties for unfair labor practices, a ban on captive audience meetings, weakening state-level "Right to Work" laws, and most controversially, an expansive definition of employment for the purposes of collective bargaining rights—the "ABC Test." The bill passed the House but was killed in the Senate by wayward centrist Democrats Kyrsten Sinema, Mark Kelly, and Mark Warner, who played the roles of corporate-backed spoilers to the brief trifecta of Biden's first Congress (as other Sun Belt Democrats had done for the previous two Democratic trifectas). Following that defeat, the administration's only subsequent progress took the form of regulatory changes through the NLRB, Department of Labor, and Federal Trade Commission that were mostly struck down by a right-wing judiciary.

The most novel, and also most revealing, aspect of labor regulation today concerns the gig economy, debate over which began during the Obama administration—a time when leading labor-affiliated researchers were downplaying its significance instead of engaging its substance. Heading into the Biden administration, there were two poles to the debate: either gig workers are employees (as the PRO Act says) and settling for anything less constitutes a sellout, or (non-)employment status should be conceded in exchange for "sectoral bargaining" and a new system of "portable benefits." The latter would effectively create a permanent two-tier system that would invite incumbent employers to replace existing workers and their unions with a lower tier of not-quite-employees rather than genuinely independent contractors, the whole thing sanctified by a paper union empowered to collect dues in exchange for the pretense of processing grievances gig employers are under no obligation to redress. Notably, both of these options end in some form of unionization.

But on both sides of this debate, actual gig workers—many of whom choose such work because they are drawn to its promise of independence and liberation from bosses—were sorely underrepresented. The pitch to workers typically made by union representatives—employment status lets you form a union, which can then negotiate a contract that gives you the protections you want, including independence—is easy for companies to organize against, not only because an independent union, let alone a contract, seems remote, but also because employers can paint union organizers as threats to worker independence. Meanwhile, the unions that play ball on the companies' terms win the prize of collecting dues in exchange for endowing the whole charade with a pro-worker gloss.

It is true that some people turn to gig work only as a last resort or in desperate conditions, when they lose access to traditional employment—as was the case when Uber got its start during the darkest days of the Great Recession. But a large number of gig workers want the ability to make a living outside an employer's supervision. That constituency would be served by a threefold agenda. First, extending the actually existing social insurance system—whose benefits are already "portable"—so that it covers them. (To be fair, some state-level enforcers have achieved this with respect to unemployment insurance during the last several years.) Second, enacting a health care entitlement that isn't tied to employment status. And third, restricting companies' ability to control the conduct of their work at a distance. But professional labor advocates are generally averse to strategies that don't culminate in unionization. So long as Democratic coalitional politics designates established unions as the exclusive spokespeople for workers and isn't pushed by bottom-up mobilization to represent or be accountable to new constituencies—including most especially unorganized and gig workers—that view will continue to prevail.

And indeed, it has led to several high-profile settlements in recent years that surrendered employment status only to set up company unions rather than confront and dismantle exploitative business models that prey on workers' desire for independence and control on the job. Running through all this was Democrats' usual tendency to see or claim a popular consensus where there actually isn't any, just because a policy mix happens to be agreed to by everyone in the room. In this case, liberal philanthropies argued that a political base for an apparently pro-worker agenda could be secured by funding GOP-aligned "policy entrepreneurs" such as Oren Cass, who touted these labor compromises as part of a working-class conservatism. The trouble was that actually existing worker constituencies simply had no seat at the table. They were treated at best as a problem to be managed.

AS FOR WELFARE, reform efforts at first had something working in their favor: the pandemic. In the midst of this structural crisis, the Biden administration did inherit a temporary expansion of the welfare state considerably more ambitious and comprehensive than anything proposed within progressive think tank circles during Trump's first term.

Before COVID-19, the prevailing anti-poverty agenda centered on the earned income tax credit and the child tax credit. These programs are popular among policy analysts for two reasons: they are tax expenditures, so there is no budget line and hence no "handout" vulnerable as a political football in appropriations fights, and they are only available to people with labor income, which effectively hands over discretion (and with it, a cut of the proceeds) to employers of low-wage workers. The push for universal basic income (UBI) that cropped up in the 2010s had challenged this paradigm—backed by Silicon Valley types claiming that the next technological innovation would lead to job losses for vast swaths of the working class, as well as by progressive policy reformers who saw it as a justified analog to the excessive capital income "earned" by the rich and documented in such detail by Piketty: a trust fund for the rest of us. Yet the established organizations, especially the Center on Budget and Policy Priorities, heavily resisted abandoning the ground they had learned to defend: that existing programs are effective (so why would we need new ones like UBI?) and that recipients of anti-poverty aid are deserving because they are workers. In the wake of this pushback, UBI advocates such as the Economic Security Project shifted the definition of their goal to include tax credit programs, recipiency of which is far from unconditional and therefore far from universal.

Then came the pandemic, which suddenly made it impossible to blame welfare recipients for not being employed. The CARES Act, passed in March 2020, included gig workers in the New Deal social insurance system (though without their employers having to pay premiums, an enormous windfall to the sector that sailed through Congress with essentially zero debate). Meanwhile, first under Trump and then under Biden, the federal government disbursed cash payments outside the logic of deservingness, to the tune of $4,000 a household or more.

Both sets of measures effectively severed the longstanding link between formal employment and eligibility for welfare. But this important ideological breakthrough didn't last, because once again no institutional infrastructure or popular consensus was built to preserve it. Quite the opposite: when employers began demanding a return to work in early 2021, they blamed pandemic welfare benefits for keeping workers at home—a bid to distract from their own shortsighted decision to lay off "non-essential" workers, dissolving employment relationships that take time and effort to re-form—to great effect. Congress and the Biden administration caved to that message.

While pandemic restrictions were broadly unpopular with the public—as was the inflation that resulted when the economy's productive capacity was suddenly unable to meet demand following all those layoffs—the pandemic welfare state emphatically was not. Nonetheless, when the Biden administration declared the pandemic over following the vaccine rollout, progressive organizations went along, and welfare policy reverted to the pre-pandemic status quo: conditional on the boss's goodwill. A great deal of laudatory ink has been spilled on Biden's economic advisors having learned Obama's lesson: too small a stimulus after the 2008 financial crisis caused political problems down the road. This time, the Democrats deliberately went bigger with stimulus. But then they reverted to business as usual, and this crisis was wasted too.

The policies that disappeared most quickly—cash payments and supplemental unemployment insurance—were precisely those missing from, indeed excluded by, the mainstream policy discussion heading into the Biden administration. Democrats could have conditioned their repeal on passing a permanent expansion of the favored policy—the child tax credit—but mustered no such leverage. The result alienated workers who experienced the height of the pandemic under Trump as a rare financial windfall and time of decreased economic stress. For them, Biden's push for Americans to "get back to work" brought back all the old problems, plus the new one of inflation.

THEN THERE IS antitrust, the policy area where the Biden administration had the greatest success. While there have been major enforcement wins—an across-the-board victory for the government in its case against Google's search monopoly; blocking some high-profile mergers on the basis that they would have harmed workers—the most significant achievement is that the reform impetus wasn't snuffed out. Despite Trump's reelection, it will almost certainly persist in academia, dedicated nonprofits, and non-federal public enforcers—not to mention among the public, which remains convinced that extractive monopolies dominate the economy and were responsible for recent inflation.

The key to this success was a willingness to depart from the old reform playbook and to take the establishment by surprise. As with tax policy, antitrust had been confined for decades to a highly arcane and technical domain—one in which dedicated practitioners were used to getting their way within very narrow boundaries of acceptable policy variation. Carl Shapiro, who served as chief economist in the Antitrust Division of Obama's Department of Justice, crystallized this attitude when he said in 2018 that the division hadn't brought a monopolization case on his watch because "there were precious few cases that warranted an enforcement action based on the facts and the case law."

But the tide turned suddenly with the advent of antitrust as a progressive priority starting in 2016, buoyed by the growing sense that major tech players did not have the public's interest at heart, as well as some insiders' search for policy levers that could be pulled through unilateral executive action. Four years later, a House Judiciary subcommittee released a report on Big Tech, laying out in great detail the actual business models of leading companies and exposing their reliance on anti-competitive practices to obtain and maintain their position. Soon thereafter Biden appointed Lina Khan, who helped lead the House investigation, and Jonathan Kanter, who had sued Google in private practice, to helm the lead enforcement agencies—the FTC and the DOJ's Antitrust Division, respectively. Unlike in tax policy, where the culture of bipartisan consensus effectively blocked reform, the pre-2016 culture of antitrust consensus worked *against* the establishment in this case, since it enabled these upstart reformers to tar everyone—Democratic and Republican staffers and academics alike—with the same compromised brush.

Yet even here, the reform effort has relied to some extent on an old pattern: marshaling credentialed experts—law professors and economists with the fanciest pedigrees and publication records—to sanctify the policy. Mobilizing a popular constituency is messy and hard; mobilizing elites was much easier, not least because proposals to this effect were likelier to win support from the progressive philanthropies leading the "post-neoliberal" charge. To this extent, the antitrust agenda too has been in keeping with the Democratic Party's elite, top-down approach to economic policy and politics in general. Its wins have not come without the cost of perpetuating a risky political strategy.

A good example is the FTC's rule banning noncompete clauses in employment. Evan Starr, the leading economist studying noncompetes, published a paper through the Economic Innovation Group after the ban was announced in 2023 exhaustively demonstrating its consistency with a recognized, well-published body of research as well as the speciousness of the economic arguments against it put forward by the Chamber of Commerce. Starr's paper is exactly the kind of thing a raft of progressive policy nonprofits are meant to produce. Nonetheless, conservative federal judges blocked the rule—one dismissing Starr's work as only "a handful of studies." The problem is that it's very easy to muddy up a scholarly consensus with motivated studies, and it's nearly impossible to convince a judge (or a congressperson) who doesn't want to be convinced that some studies are robust while others are hackwork.

Resting so much of the political burden on the power of authoritative research to structure top-down policy and persuade elites, even when the research should in fact persuade them, forgoes the option of mobilizing a popular constituency and following it where it leads, while vesting considerable veto power in experts empowered to speak authoritatively about the policy implications of their work. Tens of thousands of ordinary workers flooded the FTC with comments supporting the policy too, but the tide of public opinion made no impression on a lifetime-ensconced judiciary, all of whom are appointed thanks to their gestation in the same well-oiled right-wing political machine. Bottom-up mobilization in favor of the noncompete ban (or any other worker-friendly policy) would have meant answering the contrary judicial rulings by a call to overthrow judicial power and remove offending judges from office, but the Biden administration never even gestured in that direction or blamed the conservative judiciary for the pandemic inflation because it saw its mission as preserving faith in "our system of government," even as that system was destroying his administration.

IT IS THUS hard to see the last decade and a half as anything other than a missed, indeed wasted opportunity. The Great Recession sparked a major movement for progressive economic policy reform, and it was sustained in large part by major philanthropic gifts to progressive advocacy groups and think tanks. Asking why this agenda has come to naught is an important and necessary conversation to be having, but it is not well served by the aggressive, premature self-congratulation of the Biden administration and its allies over the last two years.

The loudest critique of the Democratic Party to have emerged in the wake of Trump's reelection is that it has become too beholden to shadow constituencies without any real popular following. There is a half-truth in this argument. The real story is that the most influential progressive philanthropic efforts on economic reform largely confined themselves to doing prestige politics as usual; when they did win a seat at the table, there was no popular base to answer to and no serious effort to build one. Instead, the "theory of change" was that intellectuals and insiders could take care of the policy and the politics would take care of itself. The result was a catastrophe out of which almost nothing lasting was achieved.

The irony is that philanthropy, in principle, should free up advocacy organizations to depart from the old rules and preexisting orthodoxy, empowering progressives to recognize which constituencies are not currently represented and activate them. And indeed, other progressive foundations have been doing just that. If reform-minded progressive philanthropy has any future, it must follow their lead, helping to grow popular movements and working in collaboration with them, rather than continue to operate solely from the inside out and the top down. ◆

Lula addresses a crowd of supporters in São Bernardo do Campo, 1989. Image: Getty Images

HOW TO BUILD A WORKERS' PARTY
Gianpaolo Baiocchi

FERNANDO MORAIS's *Lula*, a new biography of Brazil's current third-term president, describes the tension on the morning of April 7, 2018. The night before, Luiz Inácio Lula da Silva—known simply as "Lula"—had been charged with corruption and given a day to turn himself in. He'd headed to São Paulo's Metalworkers Union headquarters to discuss his next moves with a few close associates. "As the sun came up, fourteen of the twenty-four hours given by Judge Moro had come and gone," Morais writes. "They can come and get me here," Lula announces.

By that morning, the union hall has filled with union comrades, Lula's Workers' Party (PT) members, clergy, and activists from Lula's past, setting the stage for a dramatic standoff between Lula and his supporters—and by extension, ordinary Brazilians—and the powerful defenders of privilege who controlled the judiciary. Brazil's media giant, Globo, had falsely reported that Lula intended to resist arrest, and emotions are running high. At one point, there are fears that power to the union hall will be cut, and Lula's supporters discover hidden listening devices and cameras planted by police agents. Less than a kilometer away, riot police are ready to raid the building. Morais captures Lula's back-and-forth with his closest allies, some of whom urge him to flee.

The wide-ranging—and at times, politically motivated—Operation Car Wash investigation that year had implicated hundreds, including Lula and several Workers' Party officials, in systematic corruption and bribery involving Brazil's largest construction firms and Petrobras, its national oil company. Lula has maintained his innocence the whole time, but declares he will surrender to the authorities. "I would resist if I could," Lula tells São Paulo organizer Guilherme Boulos, "but I am convinced this is the best decision."

Lula turns himself in, but not before a mass is held in the union hall in honor of Marisa Letícia, his late wife, and Lula delivers a fifty-minute speech. "I dreamed that it would be possible to govern this country by bringing millions and millions of poor people into the economy, into the universities, and creating millions of jobs in this country," he says, his audience imploring him not to surrender. "They ordered my arrest, but they'll learn that the death of a fighter doesn't halt a revolution." Lula then steps into a car, but the crowd won't let it leave.

He makes his way to another waiting car, which takes him to a police station to be processed. From there, he's flown to Curitiba, where he will spend the next nineteen months in prison before being released on evidence of prosecutorial misconduct, well before the end of his nine-year sentence. Text messages exposed by a hacker had revealed collusion and manipulation in the case against Lula; eventually, he is found innocent altogether. Upon his release, he credits his supporters. "Every single day, you were the fuel of democracy that I needed," he tells them. "These people have to know one thing: they didn't imprison a man. They tried to kill an idea, and you can't kill an idea. An idea doesn't disappear."

Lula's arrest and vindication made for a spectacular drama. But it was just one of many challenges he'd had to overcome—the Car Wash incident wasn't even the first time he had been jailed by political opponents. It's hard to imagine a more extraordinary political triumph. Lula was born in abject poverty, raised mostly by a single mother, and sent to work at age eight; by adulthood, he had founded a political party. He ran for president three times before winning the fourth time in 2002 and getting reelected in 2006. After his 2022 release from prison, he won his third presidential term with the most votes—some 60.3 million—in Brazilian history.

It is impossible to reflect on Lula's life and influence without resorting to superlatives about his achievements. Barack Obama once called him "the most popular politician on Earth." At least one journalist has speculated that if you tally all the votes Lula has received across his campaigns, he might be the most voted-for human being on the planet. It seems impossible to defeat him: neither the corporate media, nor trumped-up charges and imprisonment, nor fake news and right-wing mobilization, nor even cancer and personal tragedy has put a stop to him. His very name has become a political science concept—"Lulismo"—that describes both the doctrine of conciliatory leftism he developed and a historical epoch of economic growth and unparalleled social inclusion in Brazil. Morais's book is the first to offer a detailed look at Lula's early years, from his childhood to the run-up to his first congressional election win in 1986: a period crucial to understanding the politician he was destined to become.

LULA'S POLITICAL STORY begins almost four decades before his 2018 arrest, when, in 1980, he is jailed by the military dictatorship. A former metalworker, Lula had emerged as an important, and increasingly targeted, labor leader during a wave of strikes that were galvanizing the nation as they grew. As Morais writes, Lula's response to his arrest already reflects his characteristic humor and fearlessness. When the police arrive at his house, Lula—still in bed—famously tells them, "They can go fuck themselves. I'm sleeping, damn it!" He needs to brush his teeth and have coffee before being taken in, he jokes.

The scene is gripping: Lula sits in the back of an unmarked van, flanked by six armed men, wondering if they will run him over to make his death seem like an accident—a realistic concern, given the number of activists murdered by the dictatorship in those years. Still, he musters courage. About a month later, after being held and interrogated, he is let go. If the dictatorship's goal in arresting him had been to silence him, they had badly miscalculated the power of his charisma. The arrest made Lula a cause célèbre, propelling him to national and international prominence as a symbol of the resistance and a working-class hero.

The political party Lula had helped found in February of that year, the PT, would also grow in size and influence, due in no small part to his exploding fame. Why a political outsider would choose to invest in forming a political party takes some explaining, and Morais details the evolution of both the party and Lula himself during those early years. Lula had been famous for saying that "he [didn't] like politics and [didn't] like people who practice politics," but as the one-party dictatorship started to loosen its grip on political life in the late 1970s, allowing for an official opposition party, the Brazilian Democratic Movement, it was becoming clear to Lula and others that workers would have little say or space within it. The actual idea of a Workers' Party, according to Lula, came to him on July 15, 1978, at a petroleum workers' strike in the northeastern state of Bahia.

From the outset, he was insistent that it be an authentic party of, and by, workers. "The place for students is in the schools. For priests, it's in the churches. If someone wants to create a party for workers, he has to wear overalls," he declares. Intellectuals, who would come to play a central role in the PT's future, would only come later. Mário Pedrosa, the art critic, was the first of them to join. ("The party will need people like us, at least as sympathizers," he tells a skeptical fellow intellectual.)

What an authentic party of workers would mean in practice was far from self-evident. The older Brazilian cadre left, represented by the Communist Party, as well as the armed insurrectionist movements of the 1960s, had either been obliterated or run out of the country by the military dictatorship. The socialist labor left, which some hoped would be reborn, was in disarray. The late 1970s were a heady time for a Brazilian left seeking to reinvent their political project. Though the Eastern Bloc had not yet fallen, Eastern European socialist parties were already seen as hopelessly ossified, mere apologists for statist repression.

So the PT looked inward, finding influence in liberation theology, a homegrown current of Catholicism in which salvation meant freedom from political and economic oppression, and Freirean popular education, which made critical thinking and freedom the primary goal of schooling. Social movements—urban, student, feminist, environmental—were important parts of this reinvention, too. Though the PT was founded as a mass party of workers committed to bottom-up democracy and socialism, the question of whose concerns, exactly, should be at that party's center was never foreclosed. It's unfortunate that Morais spends relatively little time on this crucial political history, choosing to focus more on capturing the larger-than-life personalities of those who attended the party meetings.

By the time the PT was officially announced at the auditorium of the Sion High School in São Paulo on February 10, 1980, it had been decided it would be an internally plural party, eschewing a strict party line. "Allowing the participation of groups with their own political ideologies and agendas and with formal representation in the directorate," Morais writes, was an innovation that was "inconceivable up to then in Brazilian and even in foreign leftist parties." The PT emerged as an often heterogeneous formation, held together by a delicate compromise, with Lula himself playing an outsized role in keeping it together.

As Brazil began its transition to democracy in the early 1980s, the Workers' Party continued to grow across the country and consolidate its strength, particularly in São Paulo. For Lula, though, the path was less clear. His first electoral attempt, running for governor of São Paulo state in 1982, was a failure, leaving him disillusioned with politics. "It hurt. It hurt a lot. I became desperate. I lost my way. I was only sure of one thing: I was done with politics," Lula admits. In 1985, a pivotal conversation between Lula and Fidel Castro during a visit to Cuba convinced him to return. As Lula reports to Morais, Castro saw an enormous victory in the election results, even though Lula had lost, and delivered an impassioned speech begging for him not to give up the fight:

> Listen, Lula: never since humanity invented the vote and invented elections, no worker . . . I repeat, no worker, no member of the working class, in any place in the world . . . has ever gotten a million votes like you did. You don't have the right to abandon politics. You don't have the right to do this to the working class.

The next year, Lula made a congressional run, winning the election with the highest number of votes ever recorded for that office, securing a seat for the PT in São Paulo state and setting the stage for his subsequent presidential campaigns. Lula's first election to the presidency in 2002 was a decided first in Brazilian history. Before then, Brazilian presidents had come from elite circles, and, even when they ran on platforms of economic inclusion—like the two presidents elected before Lula—they often bitterly disappointed the poor. In 1992, Fernando Collor left the office in disgrace in a corruption scandal; Collor's successor, Brazilian Social Democracy Party founder and sociologist (and one-time participant in early PT discussions) Fernando Henrique Cardoso managed to reduce the country's inflation, but delivered only small social programs along with increased privatization.

Lula's victory marked the culmination of over two decades of electoral organizing by the left. In his first two terms, he achieved the seemingly impossible: lifting tens of millions out of poverty through *Bolsa Família*, an income redistribution program, and an increased minimum wage. His administration nearly doubled university enrollment, and introduced aggressive affirmative action quotas for Black, Indigenous, and public school students at all the elite federal universities. In Black-majority, racially segregated Brazil, to talk about race at all—let alone recognize racial inequality—has always been taboo, but quotas have steadily transformed the middle class in the country, and, despite some opposition, are unlikely to go away anytime soon. Lula achieved all this while maintaining steady economic growth, low inflation, and reducing public debt.

Some of the accomplishments of those eight years reflected social movement and organizing demands. The Black Movement, for example, which had long fought for recognition of its claims, found a receptive audience for the first time in Brazil under Lula. The Lula administration also sponsored dozens of councils and conferences on topics like gender equality, racism, homelessness, and the needs of the youth. But ultimately, his ability to govern and deliver results was only possible because of his ability to make compromises. While Lula himself came in with a popular mandate, he did not come in with a red wave in Congress. He had to make deals in order to govern—and this meant bringing in more conservative forces and regional political machines into his coalition and government posts.

It was not a strategy without costs. Over Lula's eight years, it sometimes resulted in disappointing policies for the party's progressive base: his administration never delivered on the levels of land reform it promised nor adopted consistently pro-union positions, and it failed to confront the country's powerful economic interests—agribusiness, construction, and the media conglomerates—head-on. Lula also had to manage tensions within the PT, with some groups expecting a more consistently leftist orientation from the presidency. And while he was mostly successful at keeping the party intact, he was unable to prevent some prominent defections and the formation of splinter parties like the Socialism and Liberty Party (PSOL), now a major PT rival.

In 2005, a wide-ranging corruption scandal erupted: a number of members of Congress were caught receiving bribes to vote with the PT. Lula acted quickly to support the investigations and dismiss anyone involved, but it forever damaged the party's reputation as a party of ethical outsiders. While a number of officials from the PT's leadership were found guilty, Lula himself was untouched by the allegations and managed re-election for a second term. In 2010, after his two consecutive term limit was up, he was able to name a successor—Dilma Rousseff, his former chief of staff—and leave with an approval rating of 87 percent, the highest ever recorded in the country.

Rousseff did not fare as well. Though re-elected after a rocky first term, she faced a spiraling political crisis in which centrist coalition parties abandoned the PT. Never as able a politician as Lula, and saddled with the odious task of restricting social spending in order to manage the domestic effects of the global decline in commodity prices, Rousseff was impeached in 2015 and removed from office months later. Formally launched over a budget technicality, the impeachment was in reality a calculated attack, led by an angry and increasingly mobilized upper middle class seeking to take advantage of her lack of popularity. With Rousseff and the PT out of the way, the doors had been opened for a far-right wave: one that, in 2018, elevated Jair Bolsonaro to the presidency and a bevy of ultraconservatives to congress, inaugurating one of the darkest chapters in recent Brazilian history. During the Bolsonaro years, the government waged war on universities, science, feminists, progressive textbooks and teachers, all forms of political correctness, and the Amazon itself, accelerating deforestation to irreversible levels. And more than that, the Bolsonaro era energized violent authoritarian voices: for the first time since the end of the military dictatorship, political violence increased across Brazil.

By the time Lula assumed office again in January 2023, he had survived cancer, the death of his wife, and nearly two years in prison. His victory ended the far-right Bolsonaro regime and marked a remarkable comeback for the seventy-seven-year-old. But these events, like Lula's first two terms in office, do not make it into Morais's book, which leaves off in 1986.

THIS NEW BIOGRAPHY joins John French's excellent and incisive, if more academic, *Lula and His Politics of Cunning* (2020). It also obliquely engages with the work of André Singer, the prominent São Paulo Petista (PT supporter) and political scientist who coined the term "Lulismo" in 2009 to describe Lula's distinctive style of political compromise. Morais's book stands out for its access to its subject and the intimacy of its prose. The extensive research—hours of interviews with Lula and many others and firsthand reporting from recent events—is a monumental achievement, making *Lula* an important historical document. That its meticulous detail also makes for a compelling read is a testament to Morais's craft and Brian Mier's lively translation.

Some of the most moving chapters are the personal ones: Lula's accounts of learning to be a metalworker at technical school, being interrogated by "a polite man in a tie," the loss of his first wife at age twenty. The book doesn't pretend to be neutral—Morais openly admits his friendship with Lula in the epilogue—but in some ways, this is to its benefit, preventing an admiring tone from turning hagiographic. And *Lula* isn't aimed at the man's detractors, anyway.

In *Becoming Freud*, Adam Phillips contrasts two modes of biography writing: one that focuses on the "fanciful (i.e. wishful), novelettish setting of scenes, and thumbnail sketches of characters, with their suppositions about what people were thinking and feeling and doing," and one that delves into "the recurring preoccupations that make a life," the internal conflicts and intimate motivations. Morais excels at the first, pulling the reader into one gripping set piece after another, but this comes at the expense of the latter. We don't get a deep sense of Lula's internal life, nor the "measure of incoherence" that Phillips looks for. There is little exploration of how Lula does what he does, why he does it, or whether he wrestles with reconciling ideals with the decisions he faces as a party leader or president. Instead, Lula comes across as a sympathetic champion for Brazil's poor and working class, a man with a penchant for a good phrase, lots of charm, plenty of friends who stand by him, and a nearly inexhaustible supply of resilience and courage.

And that is a fascinating story to tell. But Brazil's troubled recent history casts a shadow over the book, one that never quite comes into view. Lula's enemies—crooked judges, police interrogators, and the corporate media—don't seem to have very complex motivations either, other than to take Lula down. The deep hatred of Lula and the left that later drove the middle and upper classes to the streets in 2013 remains a bit of a puzzle. That year, Rousseff faced protests against rises in the costs of public transportation, which morphed very quickly—and unexpectedly—into anti-government, anti-left protests. This destabilized her administration, unchaining a series of events that would lead to a legislative coup and the country's rightward turn toward Bolsonarismo a few years later. But as analysts like Singer and others remind us, Lula's administrations were quite conciliatory to capital and powerful interests. Brazil's elites did very well under him. Why would they turn on him and his project so viscerally?

Morais never tends to read Lula's early critics clearly enough to help us understand the answer to that question. But his biographical portrait foregrounds something that our analyses on the left, like Singer's, tend to underplay: the politics of recognition and dignity that Lula signifies. My own writing has tended to focus on the dynamics of the Workers' Party itself, with little attention to how Lula, the person, is seen and understood by Brazilians. Yet this is probably the biggest clue in explaining the backlash he's set off. The fact that a person like Lula—who was born poor, worked a blue-collar job, and had little in the way of formal education—could be president in such a deeply inegalitarian place like Brazil was a shock to its establishment. Lula gave ordinary people, who see themselves in him, permission to be and to want without apology. That enraged the country's elites, and it might be the most threatening thing about him.

The biography has an excellent appendix that documents the media war on Lula throughout his term in office, but it doesn't illustrate to English-language readers what many Brazilians take for granted: the open and deep class prejudice that the country's establishment and its upper and middle classes draw on when talking about Lula. He doesn't make verbal gaffes; he talks like an illiterate. It is not only that he drinks too much, but that he drinks *cachaça*, the drink of the poor. He is not corrupt; he is a common thief (*ladrão*) surrounded by grifters (*malandros*). Even the descriptions of Lula's relatively modest apartment—the supposed evidence of bribery—were tinged with outrage about how expensive the appliances were (the implication being that someone like Lula wouldn't know the difference). When good wine is served at his wedding, it is news. Brazil's elites, who go shopping in Miami and SoHo (or dream of doing so), have always been deeply embarrassed of having a president who reminds them of their gardener.

The book itself also has little to say about racial prejudice and racism, which in Brazil are never far from questions of class. Lula has been, without a doubt, "Brazil's Blackest President," in the words of José Vicente, the dean of Brazil's first predominantly Black university. It was Lula who established, for the first time, serious commercial and political ties with countries in Africa; Lula who became the first president to offer an apology for Brazil's 365 years of slavery; Lula who was the first to ever appoint Black ministers and ambassadors and whose administration created the Ministry of Racial Equality; Lula who introduced affirmative action to universities and civil service; Lula who signed the Statute of Racial Equality in 2010.

While Lula is a white man, his whiteness comes with an asterisk; he is also a migrant from the country's poorer Northeast: a *Nordestino*. *Nordestinos*, who, like Lula, migrated southward in the millions to flee poverty starting in the 1950s, are racialized in the country's richer South and Southeast. As Brazilian journalist and professor Fabiana Moraes reminds us, the elite's rejection of Lula is deeply informed by this prejudice. In 2018 he and his followers were described in major newspapers' editorials as emerging from caves in the Northeast. It was impossible not to notice the uniform pallor of Brazil's angry upper and middle classes who took to the streets in 2013, and who have since become a loyal voting bloc for the right. The electoral maps with the results from the last presidential election tell a clear story: the whiter and wealthier and more Southern the city or state, the higher the Bolsonaro vote.

Morais's next volume, which will focus on Lula's presidential terms, might be where the elements left unexplored in the first will come into clearer focus—where the contradictions of being, and becoming, Lula will be on sharpest display. These are important lessons to reflect on. But in the meantime, it is impossible to read this biography without concluding, at the end, that the world needs more Lulas. As one country after another falls to the seductions of right-wing bigotry, it is clear that opposition parties need something more than a technocratic defense of the status quo or appeals in defense of institutions that, for so many, don't work. What they need are leaders who can speak plainly to the needs of ordinary working people, and who can articulate a progressive, pro-democracy project in a way that always broadens the umbrella, as Lula has done. That he emerged in such difficult circumstances, and endured so much along the way, certainly speaks to his gifts; anyone who has ever heard him speak or been in his presence will tell you that his charisma is disarming. The way Lula himself would prefer to see it is that anyone can lead.

THE PARENTING PANIC
Aaron Bady

MY GRANDMOTHER was a good Catholic who didn't go to college and had eight children. Her oldest child went to college and had one child, me. Your own family probably fits this pattern. In a decline that correlates with education and secularism, and is concentrated in the Global North, women across the world are having about half the number of children they had only fifty years ago.

The far right sees this choice as a specific kind of crisis. While anti-abortion, anti-immigrant nationalists like J. D. Vance might not use exactly fourteen words when they rail against "childless cat ladies," they echo eugenicists like Madison Grant and Theodore Roosevelt in blaming female emancipation for "race suicide." For them, America was "great" when (white) families were large because (white) women were in the home having children, and (white) labor was cheap enough to make large-scale (nonwhite) immigration unnecessary. It does not mitigate the problem that about half of the current rate of population increase in the United States comes from new immigration; that *is* the problem.

The liberal counternarrative tends to be a smaller story, about individuals choosing not to be parents. More people are making this choice, they concede, but the important question is whether people are choosing *freely*. Are those who never wanted children—especially women historically forced into childbearing—finally free to forgo them? Or are those who *would* want children choosing not to have them, for economic or cultural reasons, or out of anxiety about a war-ridden, warming world?

However strange it may sound to characterize the post-*Roe* present as overflowing with reproductive choice, the mainstream center-left tends to agree with the far right that this choice is a *new* phenomenon, and that our predecessors were spared the existential dilemma. As Dutch philosopher Mara van der Lugt writes in *Begetting: What Does it Mean to Create a Child?*, "Traditionally, and biologically, having children was not something that is decided upon, but something that occurs." Likewise, in *What Are Children For? On Ambivalence and Choice*, Anastasia Berg and Rachel Wiseman assert that until fairly recently, having children was "not, as it is steadily becoming today, one possible path to take among several equally legitimate ones." It was "just what people did."

Books like these emphasize free choice by foregrounding a modern could-be parent (who happens to be the author, but might as well be the reader) struggling to make this incredibly consequential, and individual, decision, in the face of a society that would make that choice for her. Against her culture's repository of inherited givens and traditional foreclosures, freedom is when she discovers, *for herself,* what that right choice is. Yet what happens to "society" when it becomes the name of this "modern" problem? What if the problem isn't new? What if it isn't a problem at all?

THESE TWO BOOKS paint very different pictures of our societal backdrop. For van der Lugt, the individual faces an overwhelmingly—even oppressively—*pro*-natalist culture. As "people started having children all around me," she writes, "the question of whether I myself would want to have children suddenly seemed to become very important to other people." Because "few assumptions are so stagnant, so rigid, so deeply walled in as the assumption that the decision to have children is by default a good thing," she is invigorated when a friend suggests that having children might be fundamentally immoral, which leads her to explore the anti-natalist philosophical tradition, from Arthur Schopenhauer, Peter Wessel Zapffe, and David Benatar up to contemporary climate pessimists. Invoking Nietzsche's "parable of the madman," she argues that, as with the news that God is dead and we have killed him, people are not (generally) ready to receive the message that we can—and therefore must—choose whether to procreate, or not to do so at all.

By contrast, Berg and Wiseman see *anti*-natalism as chokingly dominant, specifically among millennials. Like "many in our generation [who] are waiting to have kids until later in life, or are forgoing it altogether," Wiseman regrets that "my mom's easy-won certainty has become harder for women like me to adopt." A desire for children "had been so available to her and yet felt so alien to me." The book has a distinct "how I learned to stop worrying" vibe, as both authors do, in the end, elect to become parents. Each chapter presents and then debunks what they take to be a plank of anti-natalist pessimism: that parenting has become unaffordable; that parenting represents patriarchal bondage; that the future has been cancelled by climate change. Each of these claims is invoked to be disputed, along with the cultural apparatus that sustains it, whether that be statistics about millennial economic well-being, a feminist tradition of maternal ambivalence novels and memoirs, or the literature of ecological collapse. For Berg and Wiseman these pessimistic narratives do damage: "Having children is steadily becoming an unintelligible practice of questionable worth," they say, that "for many people, having and raising children is no longer understood as a necessary part of a full human life."

Putting aside whether this is a bad thing, is the underlying claim true? When young people say they plan not to have children, Berg and Wiseman believe them. Yet when they assert that "natalist pressures on women in progressive and liberal secular society are lifting" and that "for many educated, working women . . . motherhood is no longer the ineluctable mandate it once was," they are speaking rather narrowly, about a very thin strand of the total population. They repeatedly reference a survey they conducted of highly educated millennials (95 percent with a college degree, almost 70 percent with a master's or higher), which is exactly the sort of pool one might expect from a survey distributed "through our social media platforms, friends, and acquaintances." After all, the most highly educated and progressive strata of society—who tend to read books like these (and reviews of them)—is where generalizations like "people are not having children today" are truest. But what makes this group of people specific is what makes it unrepresentative. About 38 percent of American millennials have bachelor's degrees, and one of the best predictors of fertility is educational status.

Berg and Wiseman have smart things to say about why highly educated people might not have children. There is surely something to their claim that a lot of climate fiction's scabrous pessimism about humanity tends to be unleavened by any sense of what's *good* about humanity and would make our extinction a tragedy. They are also probably right that feminist writers describing their ambivalence with motherhood tend not to discuss parenthood's more positive aspects. Yet one might not fault these writers for "the absence of praise of motherhood," if one didn't regard anti-natalism as, per se, a problem. After all, in contrast to childless writers like the Brontë sisters, Jane Austen, George Eliot, Emily Dickinson, Edith Wharton, Virginia Woolf, and Gertude Stein, contemporary writers like Rachel Cusk or Maggie Nelson tend to derive their maternal ambivalence from *actually being parents*. And what is more human than complaining about the misery of life (and parenting), and despairing that it's over too soon?

More to the point, using literary novels as a proxy for mass culture makes the book's focus on a strikingly narrow class of highly educated millennials all the more glaring. The cultural reach of writers like Rivka Galchen, Sheila Heti, Jenny Offill, and Lydia Millet represents a rounding error in the number of parents and could-be parents who consume mom blogs, influencer content, advice columns, parenting forums—extraordinarily popular and influential cultural forms that are almost definitionally pro-natalist.

Van der Lugt, by contrast, is less interested in the social forces that constrain choice—what Berg and Wiseman call the "externals" of climate change or economic insecurity that won't-be parents often cite—than in the ways our narratives and language foreclose choice. By anatomizing our cultural pro-natalism with an insect collector's unsentimental systematicity, her goal is "building more sensitive and sensible languages of begetting" in its place. "If there is a virtue to be associated with begetting," she writes, "it lies in making the decision to beget conscientiously and responsibly." Fair enough. Yet for all her rigor, *Begetting* can feel like a chess grandmaster playing a game against herself: neither side wins, nor ever could. We never learn if van der Lugt elects to have children, and while it feels impertinent to want to know, she opens the door with the first-person frame in the introduction. Perhaps denying us this closure is the point. Her conclusion is the kind of carefully measured and delineated position that only a philosopher could love: "not (or not yet) to say that begetting is always immoral, but that it is not always moral, and this in itself is saying a lot."

IF EVERY GENERATION thinks it invented sex, they are also wrong when they invent choosing childlessness. The fact is, outside of a very narrow, highly educated slice of the Global North, the vast majority of people today still become parents, and at roughly the same rate they always have. Meanwhile, it's worth remembering that people in the past tended to exercise the same general kinds of choice-within-constraints that we have today. The difference is in degree far more than in kind.

Books like these imply or outright state that the birthrate is falling because of a new epidemic of chosen childlessness. But the data doesn't show us that; what it shows is that people have far *fewer* children, one or two instead of eight. (Meanwhile the sharp decline in teen pregnancy alone accounts for half the drop in the United States' general fertility.) Opinion columnists and reactionary politicians habitually infer rampant childlessness from the declining number of total births, but the modern childless woman (and debates about "parents" are mainly talking about women) remains the same kind of statistical outlier she has always been.

As recently as 2016, the percentage of U.S. women between ages 40 and 44 who had borne a child was 86 percent—*higher* than it's been since the mid-1990s and down only from 90 percent in 1976, a time when only about 10 percent of women earned a bachelor's degree. The rate fell as low as 80 percent in 2006, but these are still strikingly high numbers. Direct comparisons to the past are tricky, but it's telling that in 1870, for example, only 84 percent of *married* American white women had borne a child, compared to 93 percent in 1835. (Imagine the panicked op-eds! Of course, among enslaved women, for whom reproduction was truly compulsory, the number was about 97 percent.) If we remember that perhaps 1 in 10 American women today struggle with infertility, it seems hard to imagine it could *be* much higher (at least in a reproductively free society).

The general birthrate *has* fallen, of course. But what should we compare today's figures to? Berg and Wiseman write that "after declining steadily for thirty years, the national fertility rate reached an all-time low in 2020." Yet the all-time low they refer to—1.6 live births per woman—rebounded to 1.7 in 2022, which was also the previous all-time low first reached in 1976. Isn't an "all-time low" that's lasted for fifty years better described as a half-century norm?

Indeed, if we go even a little farther back, the big picture—for two centuries—has been a steady and dramatic decline starting from an average of seven children in 1800 but culminating in just under two by the 1940s, well before the pill was invented. The postwar "baby boom" that followed was the anomalous (and temporary) spike that its name suggests, after which the United States essentially reverted back to the prior trendline. "After around 1950," Vegard Skirbekk observes in *Decline and Prosper!: Changing Global Birth Rates and the Advantages of Fewer Children*, "the pace of fertility decline in the Western countries tapered off, eventually stagnating around or just below two children per woman." Unless what you are *really* concerned with is white birthrates, immigrant populations, and women in the workplace—in the way that white panic eugenicists, a century ago, more openly admitted to being—U.S. society has already been at or below the "organic replacement rate" for essentially all of living memory (a fact that is masked by high rates of immigration).

In the transition from a high- to low-fertility society—given the massive medical, cultural, economic, and political transformations in the last fifty years (to say nothing of the last two or three centuries, or the millennia before that)—isn't the more remarkable thing that the ratio of childlessness to childfulness has changed so *little*? Even today, without a narrow focus on the segment of the population who have and exercise choice by saying no, the safe assumption is that the overwhelming majority of American women will continue to become mothers, just as they always have. Anecdotes and surveys—and airy gestures to "culture"—are often very poor guides to broader demographic trends.

It's also far from clear that people make the kind of rational, reasoned choices that our philosophers might expect of us. Take me: in my thirties, I would have described my non-parent status as a choice, but today, in my mid-forties, the census will record that I have chosen to have two children. Both of these choices are fairly typical. Millennials may choose to be childless for longer than their parents did—for a variety of obvious reasons—but when they make the opposite choice, even once, it turns out that they will be parents forever. People's choices change much more than they tend to realize, but in this respect, they only change in one direction. Survey data can only represent how people feel *now*, and while we can speculate that the future will be different than the past, there are not, yet, any good statistics on future birthrates.

At the same time, we too often underestimate the choices people had in the past, or the ambivalence they felt. My parents didn't "choose" to have a child—sometimes modern contraception fails—but, while I never asked my mother about why she hadn't wanted children, I don't think she would have told me about the panic, trepidation, or even regret that she must have felt, in 1978, as she struggled to imagine the very different life she was about to embark on. For one thing, when talking to me about it, decades later, she hoped to be a grandparent. For another, she would have told me about the life she *did* end up having. She would have assured me that I was always wanted; she would have been at pains to insist that she never regretted my existence. She would have told me one truth, but not the other one.

These are the kinds of stories parents truthfully tell their children. You don't tend to tell them what their existence cost you, or about all the other possible futures that their existence foreclosed. But my mother had good reasons to not want kids. She was the first of the eight children with which, in theory, God had blessed her parents, but who had been far more of a blessing than they had planned on. Of course, my grandparents would say they *had* chosen children; my grandmother was a good Catholic and a zealous anti-abortion activist. But the difficulty of their lives made it clear why they had not wanted *that many* children, or at least not so many so quickly. They were angry at the priests whose "rhythm method" of natural contraception delivered four children in their first four years of marriage. They felt lied to. And as the family story goes, once they had fulfilled the biblical mandate to be fruitful, they received a special dispensation from their priest to employ otherwise-forbidden contraception (after which they only had one more child). Meanwhile, my great aunt became a nun and had zero children; that, too, was a choice she made.

PEOPLE MAY *talk* more about choosing childlessness than they ever have, but contraception was not invented a generation ago. Van der Lugt references Charles Knowlton's 1832 *Fruits of Philosophy* as "one of the first contraception manuals," but in *Without Children: The Long History of Not Being a Mother*, Peggy O'Donnell Heffington observes that "there have always been reasons to opt out of motherhood, and there have always been ways to do it." The book of Genesis tells us to be fruitful and multiply, but it also specifically condemns the withdrawal method, which was at least as efficient as anything Knowlton recommended (washing out the vagina after sex with alum and vinegar). Latex condoms and the pill are certainly superior forms of contraception, but "better" is not the same as "new." Scroll through the "History of Birth Control" Wikipedia page: Isn't it a lot longer than you expected? If what we're interested in is the *choice* to become a parent—and the ethics that surround it—then what an Egyptian woman in 1850 BCE was doing, when she put honey, acacia leaves, and lint in her vagina before having sex, should be part of the conversation.

It is, of course, difficult to know how many twenty-somethings in the nineteenth century would have hoped not to have children—much less how a sexually active Silphium-user in ancient Greece would have filled out Berg and Wiseman's survey—but historians estimate that between one in six and one in three nineteenth-century pregnancies ended in abortion. This choice may have been more common in the era before it was "legalized," when it simply happened; as the province of woman, it was effectively unregulated, uncounted, and flew under the radar. It's also much easier to quantify sex that was "fruitful" than sex that wasn't. The public story of procreation tends to be told—by fathers—about the children that were had, rather than by women about the children whose existence was prevented. Yet unconceived children are still a "real" phenomenon, as a choice being made, even if it never becomes a number or a story.

For Heffington, the "choice" framing is primarily "useful for those who saw not having children as abnormal or deviant." On the right, scorn for childless women harmonizes with letting mothers sleep in the beds in which they procreated: having exercised their procreative freedom, conservatives tend to leave them to face the consequences of their choices alone. But even celebrating the free choice of women to control their reproduction—or imagining that freedom into existence where it doesn't—too often allows those with the most privileges to turn away from the many today who lack them. Fetishizing "choice" leads to triumphalism about a present whose actual freedom is neither as novel nor as evenly distributed as many imagine. As feminists of color have been saying basically forever, reproductive *justice* is far less about being able to choose than having good options to choose from.

Because she's not interested in what women *should* choose, Heffington can tell stories about how and in what conditions women *have* chosen. Nothing so simple as moral clarity emerges from her account of environmental non-procreation, for example. She writes about Paul Ehrlich's much-maligned *The Population Bomb* with rare sympathy, because explaining why the eugenicist Zero Population Growth movement linked arms with feminism in the early 1970s allows her to describe how and why they divorced. By not fetishizing choice, she can reframe infertility as perhaps "the only medical condition that is a medical condition only if the person who has it thinks it is"; indeed, by embedding the rise of reproductive medicine within the often forgotten eugenicist panic of the late nineteenth and early twentieth centuries, she can suggest that infertility's persistence as a medically untreatable problem has something to do with the fact that "people trying to solve infertility have always had other motives," whether racial uplift or pure profit.

Heffington also zooms out from the choice to conceive to the larger question of how children are cared for. Neither *Begetting* nor *What Are Children For?* says anything about the family form in which a child, once chosen, will be raised, but most readers will assume they mean biological reproduction within a nuclear family. Absent are adoption, aunties, "alloparents," professional domestic laborers, plus any of the other ways that kin is made, to say nothing of wayward lives, "polymaternalism," "mothering without mothers," and other queer, communal, blended, found, nontraditional families. These are never part of the binary choice. Yet the nuclear family is as much a modern artifact of the Global North as the drop in general fertility itself. And if you are a parent, you will perhaps understand why the expectation that children be raised in isolation from a supporting community and kin structure—that two parents raise all the children they have, all by themselves—corresponds neatly with a historical decline in the numbers of children that parents choose to have.

Indeed, Heffington argues that this "choice" is directly downstream of broader changes in social and family structure:

> In western Europe, marriage patterns began to shift in the second half of the eighteenth century, as couples increasingly struck out on their own after they wed rather than joining an extended family home, which had previously been the norm. As they did, people started controlling their fertility: having fewer kids, spacing them out in longer intervals, and stopping well before nature would otherwise have forced them to. Americans made a decisive move toward what would later be called the nuclear family around the dawn of the nineteenth century, when the individualist rhetoric of the revolution found its way into their dining rooms and hearths, and Americans pulled back from their neighbors as never before.

In some communities, these arrangements survived longer. Citing the early twentieth-century childhood of civil rights icon Ella Baker as a kind of "family socialism," Heffington describes a world "in which food, homes, family, tools, and wealth were shared by those who had more with those who had less," and "children were passed from those who birthed them to those who could care for them without anyone raising an eyebrow." She notes that "when the American anthropologist Niara Sudarkasa arrived in Nigeria in the early 1960s to study kinship patterns among Yoruba women, she found a kind of community ethos and care that shared much in common with Baker's childhood."

Yet "raising children was a communal act" for even most of white U.S. history. "American colonists of the seventeenth and eighteenth centuries 'conceived of the family almost entirely within the context of the community,'" as Heffington cites the late Helena Wall observing; if children had parents, they sometimes had more than just one or two, and their identities could change. Adoption only became "legal" in the mid-nineteenth century because, before then, it simply happened: a sister's unwanted child became yours, if she and you wanted that, and nothing more needed be said. A much more fluid sense of who children "belonged" to prevailed in a world where high-status elders had the right (and obligation) to discipline children who weren't "theirs," while the labor of parenting was just as comprehensively distributed onto a variety of (usually lower-status) women, or older children.

Unlike annual fertility and birthrate figures, there exist no press releases announcing the average number of caregivers that children have. But as nodes in a distributed network of child care, "childless" aunts, cousins, siblings, grandparents, and neighbors—who may once have had or would still have small children themselves—have traditionally been the structural foundation of high-birthrate societies, as necessary to general reproduction as those who actually bore children. Seen in this light, "childlessness" might be more of a crucial aspect of begetting than an alternative to it (something even Vance can understand, albeit in the most misogynist way possible). If the nuclear family is seen as contingent and statistically anomalous as the baby boom generation's fecundity, then history's variety of "alternative" family arrangements come to seem more like the nuclear family's penumbra, complement, and enabling context.

How did we come to think otherwise? Heffington observes that the rise of in vitro fertilization corresponds with a small but meaningful decline in adoption rates, as society has come more and more to equate parenthood with biological reproduction. But while Baker's "family socialism" is certainly not the kind of high-birthrate society that reactionary white nationalists like Vance are nostalgic for, there are many reasons why we might not want to return to the gender mores and social hierarchies that made it possible to produce large numbers of children. Do reactionaries simply romanticize high birthrates because an entire gender was excused from child care? Even in the sunniest vision of communal parenting, how many forgotten spinster aunts were forced to be nurturing caregivers in exchange for room and board because, being unmarried, they had no access to secure housing of their own? How much abuse was normalized in those arrangements?

Heffington presents a rich archive for thinking about how essential childless woman have always been into reproductive society. But how applicable is that history to the kind of problems and questions so many parents face today? With no clear social consensus on *how* to parent, the idea of fellow citizens as *co-parents* surely strikes many as an unattractive prospect. (Parenting forums are packed daily with posters angry that a stranger chided their child for self-evidently bad behavior—or wondering if they overstepped by scolding a misbehaving, unattended child.) How many progressive millennials would put their daughters in the hands of Trump-voting grandparents? Generational answers to the *how* of parenting have arguably changed more radically than the question of *whether* to be a parent. Modern parenting—especially among the well-educated—tends to treated as a psychically demanding, time-intensive, extremely difficult third job. (A much-cited 2016 study found that in 1965, mothers in Western societies spent an average of 54 minutes a day on child care activities, but that college-educated mothers in 2012 were spending an average of 123.)

My grandmother once told my mother she was selfish for having only one child; my oldest-of-eight mother told me how much of her childhood she spent taking care of her own siblings (and how my grandmother had done the same thing, as a child, when her own mother was incapacitated). This was not yet named "parentification," nor understood to be harmful to a child's development. But my mother had a different understanding about what she wanted for her child. So do I for my twins, which is typical for my demographic cohort: I would have been happy to be childless, or to have only had one, but I have never seriously contemplated having more than what demographers call the "replacement rate."

Why, after all, do we need to "replace" ourselves? Peter Thiel—Vance's patron, mentor, and donor—has warned that if everyone who can become a parent only does once, the human race will round down to zero in about a thousand years. He doesn't use the words "race suicide"; he also doesn't mention that unborn American children are, on a global scale, counterbalanced by all the African babies being born. His "we" does not include populations whose birthrate remains well over the replacement level. "Only by excluding Africa and a great many developing countries from consideration ... does the term 'baby bust' have any resonance," as Edward Paice observes in *Youthquake: Why African Demography Should Matter to the World*.

Thiel probably knows about Africa. Birthrate panics express gender through race and race through gender, and I suspect that when he bemoans "a world in which people are not reproducing themselves," it's his antipathy for Africans talking rather than his ignorance. These are also issues of labor: I suspect that Vance knows who tends to care for children like his when people like him and his wife are at work. For the highly educated, dual-income households in the Global North, whose reproduction tends to be of most concern in public discourse, lower-class immigrant women and women of color are increasingly and overwhelmingly the care workers who hold things together. For the right, they are the problem to be solved; for everyone else, they are the solution to the child care shortfall we don't tend to talk about.

IF THE United States won't throw open its borders to anyone who wants to come, another option would be for men to do more primary child care. Both modest and radical, this has the benefit of being something that is already happening.

The "traditional" gendered division of labor is often defended by a kind of biological determinism: men simply aren't *designed* for child care! For this reason, it's unsurprising that utopian feminists and family abolitionists from Shulamith Firestone to Sophie Lewis tend to see biology itself as a core part of the problem, something which must be transcended alongside everything else. Taking our reproductive "nature" seriously can feel like conceding too much to the world's Vances; modern men and women, we might think, have little to learn from a deep evolutionary past whose world was so different from our own.

The eminent evolutionary biologist, feminist, and grandmother Sarah Blaffer Hrdy sees things very differently. In *Father Time: A Natural History of Men and Babies*, she argues not only that men are much more biologically suited to be caregivers than we might have ever imagined, but—more transgressively—that there is nothing particularly "natural" about the "traditional" reproductive division of labor. Even to frame it this way, she thinks, is to fundamentally misunderstand what our nature, as humans, is. It is precisely our creation of cultures—our ability to invent and re-invent new ways to survive and thrive in a constantly changing world—that makes us the kind of animals we are, along with a radically flexible archive of latent genetic potential. Human nature, in short, is the ability to be many very different things. Biology is not a prison but a key.

A good Darwinist, Hrdy opens the book by noting she had always taken for granted, in her training (and research), how sexual selection produced a rigid division of labor between the sexes. "For over 200 million years that mammals have existed," she writes, "exclusively male care of babies from birth onward has never happened before." For this reason, "traditional" cultural expectations seemed firmly rooted in biological fact: lactation is what makes mammals *mammals*, after all, so mammalian child care is predictably a mother's affair. Especially before the industrial production of baby formula, there was essentially no alternative to breastmilk. Even today, devoted male parenting remains an exception to the rule, and precisely as associated with the urban Global North (with its dual-income nuclear households and limited options for child care) as the decline in birthrate itself.

In other words, even a trailblazing feminist biologist like Hrdy had never seriously questioned the idea that, as Margaret Mead put it, "motherhood is a biological necessity, but fatherhood a social invention." But when and where something as *evolutionarily* unprecedented as the devoted male primary caregiver has become culturally normal—even without a mother altogether—the neurophysiological facility with which men have taken to the endeavor, Hrdy argues, requires revising our scientific understanding of how parenting is gendered. What blew Hrdy's mind—much of the book is written in a first-person frame to emphasize the scientist evolving with the science—was how many *biological* responses to parenting occur in men, in response to changing social cues. As "endocrinologists documented changes in hormone levels that resembled those in mothers," she notes, "neuroscientists started to scan the brains of primary-caretaking men [and] found that their brains . . . responded the same way a mother's would."

Changes in culture and social structure may have put men "into the home," but nature was waiting for them when they got there. Not only is it possible for men's brains to respond and change in the same ways as secondary "alloparent" caretakers—the neuroendocrinological shifts most often seen with grandparents and other non-primary caretakers—but patterns associated with matrescence itself can be found in men as well, should they take on *primary* caretaker roles. (For this reason, Lucy Jones's recent *Matrescence: On Pregnancy, Childbirth, and Motherhood* contains a section on men, covering much of the same science.) What makes the greatest difference, it turns out, is not gender—nor even childbirth and lactation, though they do make *a* difference—but time: the longer a man spends in intimate caretaking proximity to an infant, the more this "father time" will rewire his brain. At her most utopian, Hrdy ventures to suggest that a world of nurturing dads would represent more than just the tapping of an untapped labor resource; if, as many people say, so many of our social problems boil down to men being *men*, a different biological constitution of masculinity represents a revolutionary shift in human society.

Much of *Father Time* is devoted to the story of why scientists never bothered to investigate this possibility. Since Darwin, when patriarchal scientists looked to our primate relatives to understand what was "natural" for humans, they saw mammals for whom paternal care was extremely unusual and drew the congenial but erroneous conclusion that women were simply evolved to do child care in ways that men were not. But as even Darwin noticed (though promptly forgot, as Hrdy points out), human beings share a great deal, genetically, with our hermaphroditic fish ancestors, and that library of genetic potential matters. While neuroscientists often privilege the most distinctively human neural regions, in the cortex, so many of the things we do the most—eat, sleep, mate, and parent—do not derive from our proudly *Homo sapiens* heritage. These oldest and most "animal" behaviors tend to be governed by the hypothalamus, where we are most like our most distant and fishy ancestors.

Hrdy contends we are now in an evolutionary moment where the relationship between genes and phenotypes is being radically revised. Citing Mary Jane West-Eberhard's wasp studies, she observes that genes are often the "followers rather than the initiators of evolutionary change"; rather than the kind of "operating system" that an analogy with computer code would suggest, our genes might be better understood as a toolkit of inherited and latent possibilities for organisms to draw from as the world around them changes. Nothing is more natural, in other words, than for what is "natural" in a species to change (and to do so by reviving genetic possibilities that we might tend to associate with our non-primate evolutionary ancestors). When the world is changed—or when we've changed the material conditions of the world in which we reproduce—our "nature" is to evolve to thrive in our new context.

What *does* make humans at least somewhat unique, among primates, is that we are *particularly* hardwired for culture, for building self-replicating societies that develop and teach social responses to changing environmental conditions. These cultures may change faster than the range of options our genes provide for us to pull from, and fathers and mothers do not, in a biological sense, parent in *precisely* the same ways. But if we are "supremely indoctrinable apes," it makes no sense to describe our cultures as *opposed* to nature. It is our nature to be enculturated, just as the function of our cultures is to push our nature forward, creating biologically distinct forms of human being as a result of our integration into ever-changing environments.

At the highest level of generalization, Hrdy tells an evocative and compelling—if basically speculative—story about how learning to nurture made us human. Babies gave us culture, she argues, because they taught us empathy and socialization: "in the process of growing up reliant on eliciting care from others as well as mothers ... little humans began to develop their inordinately other-regarding sensibilities." It was in the harsh Pleistocene conditions where our branch of the mammalian tree formed that infants first learned to cultivate caretakers *other* than their biological parents; as they became effective and empathetic charmers, adults, in turn, developed new capacities to be charmed by children who were not their own. Perhaps, Hrdy suggests, this is how we learned to imagine ourselves collectively, and to behave as if the well-being of other children than our own was also important. It may even be that as we transformed ourselves into caregivers, we created modern human society as we know it.

Maybe we'll do it again. As we face the dawning of a climate-changed world, defined by very different environmental conditions than for literally all of recorded human history—an almost unspeakably omnipresent context for all of these books—one response to what is coming is to stand athwart history and call for a return to whenever or whatever we take to be the moment when things were *normal*, or what we once expected normal to be. What I take from Hrdy's much more expansive view of human possibility is a strange sort of confidence in futures we've never seen or imagined. Perhaps this is her perspective, as a grandmother who has seen the world change so much, rather than a millennial faced with the sudden prospect that it will. But of course the world will end, and begin again, just like it always has. Like dying and being born, it's what makes us what we are.

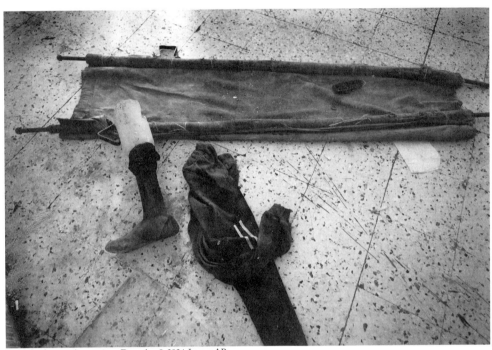
Syria's Saydnaya military prison, December 9, 2024. Image: AP

SYRIA'S "HUMAN DEBRIS"
Joelle M. Abi-Rached

IN THE FALL of 1997, I took part in my first protest—a student demonstration in Beirut. At the time, Lebanon was controlled by the late Syrian president Hafez al-Assad, father of the recently ousted Bashar al-Assad. Like other students, I was appalled by the ruthlessness of his rule. During its nearly three decades of occupation (1976–2005), the Syrian regime assaulted, kidnapped, tortured, and killed those who opposed its diktat, including journalists, intellectuals, artists, and politicians. It also censored every aspect of our lives. Books were banned; films were censored; public talks were prohibited, and independent broadcasting was either heavily monitored or outright forbidden.

The protest I attended was held at the Université Saint-Joseph, founded by French Jesuits in 1875 and run in the 1990s by a Lebanese Jesuit. I remember that day vividly. The Faculty of Law and Political Science's entrance on *rue Huvelin* was surrounded by hundreds of security officers, *mukhabarat* (the dreaded intelligence services), and other armed henchmen. The only thing that separated us from them was the gate of the university and the black soutane of the Jesuit rector, who was trying to talk the men out of entering the campus and arresting us. I don't remember how the protest ended, but in retrospect, I think the Jesuit father was trying to buy us time. I managed to escape with other students through a back exit.

Today I write from Beirut, not far from that gate of the university. This time, however, I find myself witness to a transformative moment in Syria's history and perhaps even the region. On December 8, thirteen years after peaceful pro-democracy protests gave way to a devastating civil war that consolidated Assad's brutal regime, the Syrian opposition, led by Abu Mohammed al-Jolani and the rebel group Hayat Tahrir al-Sham (HTS), entered the Umayyad Mosque in Damascus, bringing an end to the Assad family's five-decade rule.

It is no coincidence that al-Jolani—now known by his real name, Ahmed al-Sharaa—chose this mosque to declare the triumph of the Syrian revolution. The first Muslim dynasty to establish a vast empire, the Umayyads began building their mosque in 705 to rival the grandeur of Roman and Byzantine religious monuments, reflecting the caliphate's ambitions and legitimacy as a new empire. Their rule marked a major transition to a new regime—a bridge between the early Islamic period and the later caliphates—and institutionalized many aspects of governance and administration that became hallmarks of Islamic empires. The mosque also houses relics of John the Baptist, or Prophet Yahya, as he is known in Islam. It is built on the site of a Byzantine church, itself constructed on a temple dedicated to Baal

Hadad, the Semitic god of storms, thunder, and rain. It stands as a living symbol of the layers of history, culture, and religious diversity in the Middle East.

The site is meaningful in another sense, as well. It was sheer force and an Islamist ideology, not the secular and peaceful opposition movement that had launched a revolution in 2011, that successfully liberated Syria from the Assad regime. And, yet, like the Umayyads, al-Sharaa now speaks of the "transition" to a "new Syria." Claiming that HTS has moved on from its jihadist past, he has vowed to govern with inclusivity and respect for Syria's diverse society.

Many are skeptical. Some members of the transitional government have already sparked outrage over their views on women. Meanwhile, rebel groups have fragmented, with different factions governing different parts of the country, variously influenced by other powers—Iran, Russia, Turkey, Israel, and the United States among them. Then there is the question of free elections. In late December Al-Sharaa emphasized the importance of establishing security and stability and the need for a "comprehensive population census" before holding them. While he acknowledged what previous movements overlooked—that drafting a new constitution requires time and a clear vision for a new social pact—others view this delay with distrust. It remains to be seen how the transitional authorities will govern a country devastated by war, sanctions, corruption, and an economy in ruins.

Despite the anxieties and uncertainties about the path ahead, one thing is clear: HTS's victory has starkly exposed the murderous, paranoid, and barbaric nature of the Assad regime. The task of rebuilding a just and inclusive society in the aftermath of such unfathomable state violence may prove to be its greatest challenge.

ONE OF THE first acts of the Syrian rebels was to liberate prisons across the country, allowing the world to bear witness to Assad's crimes. The first wave of emotions—joy and anger mingled with horror—emerged from the liberated Saydnaya prison, notorious for housing political and military prisoners and often described as a "human slaughterhouse."

Videos posted to social media show thousands of prisoners being freed from medieval-like cells, including children and women. Thousands had been confined, deprived of light for decades. Haunting images of the liberated—emaciated and broken—draw chilling parallels to the liberation of Nazi concentration camps. Gaunt figures, lost and disoriented, unable to recall even their own names, spill out. Other tortured bodies were discovered in the morgue, some so severely tortured that they were unrecognizable by their relatives. Thousands were still unaccounted for—many likely cremated in a nearby crematorium. The White Helmets, a humanitarian group that assisted in the rescue efforts of the detainees, observed "bodies in ovens" and reported that daily executions took place within the complex. Piled bodies showing signs of unimaginable torture from Saydnaya were dumped in other hospital morgues, including the Harasta military hospital in Damascus's countryside.

The numbers of released prisoners and bodies discovered pale in comparison to the more than 130,000 people who had been imprisoned across Syria, according to the Syrian Network for Human Rights. On December 9, the director of this independent human rights organization, founded in 2011 to document the atrocities of the regime, broke down on live television after announcing that most of the forcibly disappeared should be presumed dead.

As prisons were liberated, mountains of files were uncovered—in one instance, stacked high at the politburo in the city of Suwayda, where it seemed that every family in the city had a dossier. There are likely many other such bureaucratic warehouses throughout the country, as if lifted straight from Kafka. Unlike in *The Castle*, however—and *pace* the new de facto governor of Damascus—Syrian bureaucracy has had direr consequences than inefficiency, alienation, and corruption. It was a tool of repression, a mechanism for consolidating authoritarian power, and the glue that kept this ruthless regime in place.

Paradoxically, state bureaucracies have often documented their own crimes. In Nazi Germany, the Shoah was meticulously documented, from train schedules for deportations to records of executions. In Cambodia, the Khmer Rouge kept detailed documentation on prisoners, including photographs and confessions, at facilities like Tuol Sleng, today the site of the Tuol Sleng Genocide Museum. In Latin America, despite government efforts to conceal methods of repressing those labeled as "subversive" during the so-called "dirty wars," dictatorial regimes left behind troves of archival traces, even as significant gaps and silences persist. Over the last decade, detailed records of detainees, torture, and executions have been leaked from

Syria, too. In 2013 alone a former Syrian military forensic photographer, using the pseudonym "Caesar," smuggled thousands of photographs out of Syria—images from the state's own intelligence and security agencies that document the deaths of more than 11,000 detainees between 2011 and 2013.

After being entrusted with the Caesar files, Human Rights Watch published a damning report in 2015 entitled *If the Dead Could Speak*. Three years later, Amnesty International reported evidence of widespread torture, starvation, beatings, mass hangings, and disease in Saydnaya as well as other Syrian government detention facilities. The United Nations Special Envoy for Syria, Geir Pedersen, who visited the liberated prison in Saydnaya last month, was met with angry relatives of prisoners outraged by the UN's inability to secure access to the prison or demand accountability—despite several reports and statements by the Independent International Commission of Inquiry on the Syrian Arab Republic over the past decade.

SINCE DECEMBER 8, numerous mass graves have been uncovered in Syria, confirming Caesar's crucial assertion that his forensic documentation represented "only a snapshot in time, geography, and place." The International Commission on Missing Persons in The Hague said that there may be as many as sixty-six mass graves of political prisoners throughout the country. In al-Qutayfah, 40 kilometers north of Damascus, as many as 100,000 bodies have been discovered. According to various accounts from locals, everyone had known for years what was happening there, yet the fear of repercussions kept them silent—except perhaps for the town's former mayor, who was detained after refusing orders to construct a mass grave.

"We really haven't seen anything quite like this since the Nazis," said Stephen Rapp, former Ambassador-at-Large for War Crimes Issues and head of the Office of Global Criminal Justice at the U.S. State Department, on a visit to al-Qutayfah last month. Having previously led prosecutions at the Rwanda and Sierra Leone war crimes tribunals, Rapp is now collaborating with Syrian civil society to document evidence of war crimes and assist in preparations for potential future trials.

The Nazi reference should not be taken lightly. In an interview in December, historian Uğur Ümit Üngör, coauthor of *Syrian Gulag: Inside Assad's Prison System* (2023), observed that some of the methods of torture used in Saydnaya, such as the *falaka* (striking soles with a stick), were adopted from the Ottomans, while others, like electrocution, were borrowed from the French in Algeria. But still others appear to draw direct inspiration from Nazi practices. A major exposé published in 2017 in the French quarterly *Revue XXI* highlighted the crucial role played by Alois Brunner, the "Nazi of Damascus," as the two journalists who broke the story, Mathieu Palain and Hédi Aouidj, called him. Eichmann's right-hand man, Brunner was responsible for killing 130,000 Jews and eluded capture after World War II. He died in Damascus in 2001 and was reportedly instrumental in advising the Syrian regime on torture, interrogation, and extermination methods.

The similarities with the Nazi methods are indeed uncanny. One common mode of torture used an iron press that literally crushed people to death. Another notorious method, known as *bisat ar-reeh* ("flying carpet"), involves strapping detainees to a wooden slab that is then folded until their spine cracks. (Moaz Mor'eb, a reporter who covered the U.S. invasion of Iraq, and who was arrested upon returning to Syra and imprisoned for eighteen years, described enduring various torture methods including the dreadful *bisat ar-reeh*, which he said was designed to break a person completely, both physically and morally.) Most harrowing are the cells where torturers could release a type of gas to kill prisoners.

Nevertheless, the liberation of Saydnaya has revealed something more perverse and complex than the "banality of evil," as Hannah Arendt described the way Nazis carried out their crimes with the diligence of mindless bureaucrats. Blending Stasi-like practices with Soviet-style repressive methods, the Syrian bureaucracy did not merely monitor dissenting behavior to enforce accountability and obedience. It deployed "barbaric" means of extreme violence and fear as tools of governance, as Michel Seurat argued in his important work, *Syrie: L'État de barbarie* (1989). (The book was published a year after he died in captivity at the hands of the Islamic Jihad Organization, the precursor to Hezbollah, during the Lebanese civil war.) Moreover, many of these bureaucrats sustained authoritarianism through ties of blood, sect or ethnicity making resistance all the more difficult. The state security apparatus was so pervasive and perverted that it coerced family members into informing on one another, turning neighbors against neighbors and families against their own.

Some political prisoners freed in early December spoke of unimaginable horrors. Other stories were simply miraculous. Many faced arbitrary arrest—among them Amjad Baiazy, a friend I know from our time studying in London. He disappeared for three months at the start of the 2011 revolution, swept up in the regime's widespread crackdown, and was detained in one of the security prisons notorious for torture. According to a message he sent me in December, he was charged with defaming the regime and "weakening national sentiment."

Raghid al-Tatari was a twenty-seven-year-old pilot when he was imprisoned in the early 1980s. His crime: refusing to bomb Hama where Assad père brutally repressed an uprising by the Muslim Brotherhood, killing tens of thousands of people. Suhail Hamwi, a Lebanese citizen (one among 9,000 Lebanese believed to have been forcibly disappeared in Syria), spent thirty-three years in various prisons, including Saydnaya. His crime: "collaborating with the Lebanese Forces" (a Christian political party critical of the Syrian regime), as he stated in an interview. Taken from his home, he left behind his eleven-month-old son and only last month returned to see his grandchildren. In an interview following his liberation, he stated that one should not ask about suffering, because, "Everything there is suffering—the air you breathe carries the taste of it, and even your dreams, the last private and free space left to you, are consumed by despair and suffering." His words remind me of what Frantz Fanon called "atmospheric violence, this violence rippling under the skin." And these are only a few stories among thousand other political prisoners who were freed that day—to their disbelief.

Prominent activist Mazen al-Hamada, one of the faces and voices of the revolution and the living archive of Assad's torture machine, was hanged days before the liberation of Saydnaya. His body was found in the morgue of the prison with signs of torture. In a powerful documentary released last year, *Syria's Disappeared*, you can see him, while living in political asylum in the Netherlands, breaking down in tears on camera, saying soberly, "The law will hold them accountable. I won't rest until I bring them to court and achieve justice." Remarkably, he decided to return to Syria in 2020—a move that underscores the weight of his convictions and the risks he was willing to take. But like the historian Marc Bloch and countless others who were executed by the Nazis just before the liberation of death camps, he did not live to see the collapse of "Assadism," as Syrian intellectual Yassin al-Haj Saleh prefers to call the Baathist regime. French president Emmanuel Macron recently announced that Bloch will be interred at the Panthéon. Will Syria ever have a Panthéon to honor its intellectuals, artists, activists, and ordinary citizens with a conscience—those who were so coldly and horribly executed?

This brutal context explains why many feared that the Syrian revolution that began in 2011 could not possibly succeed. Among them was al-Haj Saleh himself, who spent sixteen years in Assad's prisons after being arrested while studying medicine in Aleppo and whose wife Samira Al-Khalil was forcibly disappeared by an extremist Islamist armed faction in 2013. In his poignant book *The Impossible Revolution* (2017), he describes the Syrian uprising as both an extraordinary act of defiance and an insurmountable struggle against a deeply entrenched system of power, corruption, and violence. While he embraced the revolution's ideals, he believed their realization would be elusive.

AS PANKAJ MISHRA has noted, Israel's first prime minister, David Ben-Gurion, saw Holocaust survivors as poor material for the new Jewish state, calling them "human debris." "Everything they had endured," he thought, "purged their souls of all good." To Ben-Gurion these wounded and deeply broken individuals were obstacles to his vision of the land of milk and honey.

Yet, Shoah survivors endured—though some, overwhelmed by the guilt of surviving and the weight of living in a world that had largely abandoned them, chose suicide. Their suffering spurred the emergence of trauma studies and brought greater understanding to the deep intergenerational effects of state violence, oppression, discrimination, racism, and genocide.

Witnessing today the overwhelming destruction of all institutions that sustain life in Gaza, the systemic oppression by Israel through the imprisonment and torture of thousands of Palestinians (most notoriously in Sde Teiman and Ofer), the destruction of lives and livelihoods in south Lebanon, and now this grotesque naked state violence in Syria, I cannot help but wonder how these "brutalized" and traumatized societies will ever heal. Are they the "human debris" Ben-Gurion condemned, or can we, even amid so much ruin, devastation, and abysmal moral decay, imagine seeds of hope and positive change? Are we doomed to repeat the traumas of the past? Will trauma beget more traumas? What kind of reconciliation can Syrians pursue while embracing the imperative of Holocaust survivors to "forgive but not forget," making remembrance a moral and historical duty?

Historical traumas are deeply interwoven, with far-reaching legacies. As the Sunni majority now turns against the Alawi minority that has ruled Syria for decades, many observers have warned the country will go the way of Libya or Iraq and face civil war. Must these historical patterns be our destiny? We should ask how a society fractured by violence and oppression can heal, confront its painful past, and address a litany of unresolved traumas: from the Hama massacre in 1982 (10,000–40,000 killed) and the 2013 Ghouta chemical attack (over 1,400 killed, including many children) to the more than 100,000 forcibly disappeared and thousands executed in Saydnaya prison, to say nothing of the Syrian regime's brutal occupation of Lebanon. Al-Sharaa has been notably cautious in recent weeks, acknowledging Assad's role in assassinating Lebanese opposition figures but framing it as a matter of the past. And while asserting that the new Syria would refrain from "negative interference" in Lebanon, he also signaled the need to address the lingering issue of Islamists in Lebanese prisons.

As the prominent (and dearly missed) Syrian philosopher Sadiq Jalal al-Azm once argued, the war in Syria has been primarily waged by a murderous state against its own people, whom it regards "as no more than rabble—ignorant, backward, unprepared for democracy, and undeserving of liberty of any sort." To the Syrian regime, the people were brutes to be silenced at any cost. The rationale was one of extermination, in line with the genocidal logic of settler colonial empires, so powerfully described in Sven Lindqvist's book, "*Exterminate all the Brutes.*" After all, the regime's infamous slogan, "Al-Assad or we burn the country," mirrors another, "après moi, le déluge" (after me, the flood), attributed to King Louis XV of France. Both prioritize the ruler's self-preservation and threaten inevitable chaos in their absence; they serve simultaneously as an *ex ante* means to terrorize opposition and an *ex post* self-fulfilling prophecy.

IT IS NO EXAGGERATION to say that Syria's path forward could shape the future of the entire region. After the fall of Saddam Hussein, Iraq—under the direct interference of the United States—opted for a "de-Baathification" campaign to purge the administration, police, and security forces of people formerly affiliated to the Baath party. The policy had disastrous consequences, fueling violence, sectarianism, governance failures, and the alienation of a significant portion of the population. Meanwhile, merely two years after the killing of Muammar Gaddafi in 2011, the General National Congress in Libya voted for a "Political Isolation Law" banning all officials who ever worked with him. This too had dramatic consequences on the democratic transition, deepening the divisions in Libyan society.

Perhaps learning from these catastrophic results in Iraq and Libya, HTS has granted a general amnesty for low-ranking officials and all military personnel who had been conscripted under the Assad regime while pledging to create special tribunals for high-ranking officials and others who have "committed crimes against Syrians." The UN has called for "the humane treatment of ex-combatants," and the preservation of all evidence and crime scenes, including mass grave sites, to ensure that justice can be served. In the past few weeks, it has swiftly intensified its commissions and documentation of atrocities, already compiling a list of 4,000 perpetrators of human rights violations in the hope of securing accountability at the highest levels.

The Syrian "transition" has so far been relatively bloodless, with only a few isolated incidents of revenge killings and attacks. But will this be enough to forge a new social pact, the "rebirth of the republic" that al-Azm hoped for in a 2014 essay in these pages, two years before his passing? How will the Syrian people, who have endured so much suffering, find a path to healing? How do we think about the deep traumas inflicted on populations where violence and fear serve as the currency of the ruling political class and its security apparatus? What of those who were raped, humiliated, tortured to death, and mutilated—and of those who inflicted these unimaginable acts of violence and terror on their fellow citizens?

Although imperfect and challenging, there are models available as Syria's new rulers take on the enormous task of uniting the polity. In *A Human Being Died That Night* (2003), South African psychologist Pumla Gobodo-Madikizela, who served on South Africa's Truth and Reconciliation Commission (TRC), concludes that the only way to overcome the inevitable tension between the need for justice and the need to move on is through forgiveness—not as an act of grace, but as a means to reclaim agency and break the cycle of violence. Of course, the goal of such reconciliation efforts is not simply individual healing, though many former victims have testified to its efficacy in this regard. Rather, such efforts must be coupled with far-reaching structural, institutional, and economic reforms to achieve a truly inclusive and sustainable future. It is important to remember that while the TRC was instrumental in preventing mass violence and fostering a sense of accountability for past atrocities, it fell short of addressing the entrenched inequalities and toxic political economy that have defined post-apartheid South Africa.

In other cases, tribalism and violence have persisted. Following the 2011 Tunisian revolution that ousted President Ben Ali, a Truth and Dignity Commission was meant to address past human rights abuses, corruption, and political repression under the country's post-independence authoritarian regimes ultimately fell short of achieving meaningful accountability—partly due to its rejection by political elites, many of whom were tied to the former regime or had benefited from its corruption. And in Algeria, the lack of a truth and reconciliation commission reflects a deliberate choice to avoid addressing its complex and painful history. Psychoanalyst Karima Lazali has argued that the failure to address colonial and post-independence trauma—so powerfully documented by Fanon—is eventually mirrored in the fragmentation of the polity.

In the end, Syria's victims of unthinkable brutality are neither "human debris" nor "natural" prophets of hope and radical change. Whether Syria can become a model of inclusion in a region plagued by sectarian tensions, what Ibn Khaldun called *asabiyyah* (or tribalism), and the ever-present specter of neo-imperial rivalries, will depend on its commitment to justice, its ability to foster genuine reconciliation, and the establishment of participatory governance that addresses deep-rooted social and political wounds.

THE REALITY OF SETTLER COLONIALISM
Samuel Hayim Brody

CHRISTOPHER NOLAN'S FILM *The Prestige* presents a three-act structure said to apply to all great magic tricks. First is the pledge: the magician presents something ordinary, though the audience suspects that it isn't. Next is the turn: the magician makes this ordinary object do something extraordinary, like disappear. Finally, there's the prestige: the truly astounding moment, as when the object reappears in an unexpected way.

Poet and literary critic Adam Kirsch, author of the recent book *On Settler Colonialism: Ideology, Violence, and Justice*, doesn't present himself as a magician. But there is no denying that he is a master rhetorician, putting his talents to work in repeated sleights of hand. The purpose of the book is to relieve its readers of the sense that there is anything respectable about the central topic of discussion. Judging by an unfortunate review from Michael Walzer that appeared in the *Jewish Review of Books*, which more or less thanks Kirsch for doing the reading so he doesn't have to, *On Settler Colonialism* is already working its magic, and I am afraid that it will continue to provide this public disservice for years to come. Its ultimate goal: to make the idea of settler colonialism disappear.

"Settler colonialism" falls into the category of concepts that may provoke guilt in a certain type of liberal and fury in a certain type of conservative. For liberal nationalists, including liberal Zionists like Kirsch, the typical response is something in between: a defensive fragility. Like "gender performativity" and "critical race theory," settler colonialism was until fairly recently the province of a relatively small academic field, though it has now broken containment and entered the world of public discourse (losing something in translation, as such breakthroughs always do). The basic idea of settler colonialism is that in addition to classic colonialism, in which a wealthy and powerful country establishes military and economic control over a weaker one to extract its resources, there is also another type, in which settlers arrive with the goal of taking over the land completely, evicting, displacing, or eliminating the native peoples. Paradigmatic examples of the former are France in Indochina and Britain in India; paradigmatic examples of the latter are the United States, Australia, Canada, and New Zealand.

If this seems reasonable or uncontroversial to you, well, that's why the field of settler colonial studies wasn't immediately a lightning rod from the moment of its founding in the 1990s. Arguments over the taxonomy of colonialism according to regime type and political economy can be dry stuff. The ideas of settler colonial studies have been slowly taken up in varying degrees by other fields, from history and anthropology to Indigenous studies, but what makes it a hot topic now is the highly visible public inclusion of another country in the category: the State of Israel.

Arguments to this effect are nothing new in themselves. Palestinian intellectuals like Fayez Sayegh made the comparison first but were scarcely heard in the West. Later, the French-Jewish historian Maxime Rodinson, whose parents were murdered in Auschwitz, published an article entitled "Israël, fait colonial?" ("Israel, a colonial fact?") in June 1967, just as the Six-Day War resulted in the conquest of the West Bank and Gaza Strip from Jordan and Egypt. As Kirsch discusses, Rodinson, an anti-Zionist who believed the Palestinians had suffered unjustly, nonetheless warned against the Algeria comparison. Unlike the French *pieds-noirs*, the first Israelis had no mother countries to return to. They may have been colonizers, Rodinson argued, but they were not agents of empire; they may have been conquerors, but they were first refugees.

This, you might think, is just the sort of analysis that leads scholars to coin new terms and create new categories. So what's wrong with "settler colonialism," which exists precisely for this purpose? Kirsch begins to answer this question with his initial sleight of hand, on the very first page of the book. As Michael Caine's character in *The Prestige* describes the pledge: "The magician shows you something ordinary: a deck of cards, a bird, or a man. He shows you this object. Perhaps he asks you to inspect it to see that it is indeed real, unaltered, normal. But of course, it probably isn't."

Kirsch presents us with several seemingly alarming statistics from a Harvard/Harris poll of registered voters taken two months after the brutal attacks of October 7, when 1,195 people were killed (including 815 civilians) and 251 taken hostage. Among respondents aged

18 to 24, 66 percent agreed that Hamas's assault was "genocidal in nature." Yet 60 percent also said the attack "can be justified by the grievances of the Palestinians." These numbers may cry out for explanation, as public opinion surveys so often do, but Kirsch's interpretation strains credulity: he writes that "more than half of college-age Americans seem to believe that it would be justified for Palestinians to commit a genocide of Israeli Jews."

Kirsch doesn't inform us that the poll reached only 150 people in the age bracket he cites. He doesn't consider that their broad agreement with the claim that the attacks were "genocidal in nature" might indicate their *lack* of support for genocide. Nor does he mention that the poll found overwhelming—80 percent—support among this group for the view that Israel "has a right to defend itself against terror attacks by launching air strikes on targets in heavily populated Palestinian areas with warnings to those citizens," as well as 58 percent support for the view that Hamas "needs to be removed from running Gaza." Most notably, Kirsch fails to mention more reliable polls conducted around the same time that yielded very different results. A Generation Lab poll of college students that reached more than 900 people found that 67 percent of those who were aware of the attack called October 7 "an act of terrorism," compared with just 12 percent who found it a "justified act of resistance." Meanwhile, a Pew Research survey of over 12,000 people found that 58 percent of 18- to 29-year-olds reached called Hamas's methods "unacceptable," compared to only 9 percent who found them "acceptable."

Nevertheless, having supposedly established the genocidal tendencies of American college students en masse, Kirsch spends the next few pages lining up citations from academics and activists seeming to praise or at least equivocate on the October 7 attacks. These include references to Israel's settler colonial nature. Kirsch concludes, on this basis, that it is the "ideology of settler colonialism"—a phrase he coins but never defines—which leads these critics to be so insensitive to the value of Israeli Jewish life. But Kirsch never actually *argues* this fundamental claim, on which the rest of his book rests. This oversight is both fascinating and dismaying. Rather, he allows the sequence of his presentation to lead the reader to the conclusion that "for many academics and activists, describing Israel as a settler-colonial state was a sufficient justification for the Hamas attack," and he then proceeds as if genocidal hatred and violence against settlers is the inevitable consequence of any talk of settler colonialism.

Let us not mince words. Some people, including some who refer to Israel as a settler colonial state, have indeed made statements to the effect that "there are no civilians in Israel." But by the same token, self-declared Zionists, Christian as well as Jewish, American as well as Israeli, have for decades made statements to the effect that Israel is "fighting human animals" and that "there are no civilians in Gaza." If the former in itself counts as evidence of a dangerous "ideology of settler colonialism," surely the latter must count as evidence of a dangerous "ideology of Zionism"? Needless to say, Kirsch identifies no such thing. For all his outrage at justifications of genocidal violence, he fails to quote, much less condemn, a single example of such speech—including the statements made by Israel's political and military leaders that South Africa cites in its case charging Israel with genocide at the International Court of Justice. Perhaps that is because Kirsch understands that if "rhetorical ferocity" (as he calls it) is the standard of argument, he has no leg to stand on.

The game is given away in claims like "the killing of Israeli civilians was welcomed by many Palestinian sympathizers." Swapping the words "Israeli" and "Palestinian" in this sentence yields a claim that is equally true, but Kirsch never once uses the phrase "Palestinian civilians" in the book, much less makes reference to any of Israel's violations of international law. The function of this rhetoric is quite plainly not to analyze but to scandalize us into demonizing "Palestinian sympathizers," especially those on college campuses. Yet serious analysis must look beyond speech acts to objective conditions, including the basic facts that Israel is the dominant and only nuclear power in a deeply asymmetric conflict, exercising almost complete control over Gaza's borders, airspace, and territorial waters since 2005; that many thousands more Palestinian civilians have been killed by Israel than the other way around; and that millions of Palestinians remain stateless most proximately because Israel's strongest ally—the United States—is a global hegemon that holds veto power in the UN Security Council, which it used to deny Palestinian statehood as recently as last April. If Kirsch had read Frantz Fanon more carefully than his review of Adam Shatz's recent biography indicates, he might have recognized that the "vengeful" attitudes expressed on both sides of the conflict are exactly what theories of settler colonialism predict will arise in such circumstances.

Another sign of Kirsch's evasiveness lies in the phrase "the Hamas attack" itself, which is used throughout the book but never distinguishes between attacks on soldiers and military installations and attacks on civilians. It is true that many more civilians than soldiers were harmed and killed on October 7. But it is also obvious enough why Kirsch fails to draw this distinction: doing so might cloud the dehumanizing picture he intends to paint of Palestinians who support violent resistance—the very thing he accuses the "ideologues of settler colonialism" of doing to all Israelis. By conflating "attack" with "attack on civilians," Kirsch not only overinterprets the evidence he cites of support for the October 7 attacks; he means to suggest, without having to make an argument, that there can be no moral or legal basis for Palestinian armed conflict with Israel whatsoever. Yet so many pre-state Zionists, from David Ben-Gurion to Ze'ev Jabotinsky, would have agreed in principle with the UN General Assembly's 1982 resolution affirming "the legitimacy of the struggle of peoples for independence, territorial integrity, national unity and liberation from colonial domination, apartheid and foreign occupation by all available means, including armed struggle." Clear-eyed, serious reflection on this issue would have contributed a great deal to public discussion, but Kirsch offers nothing of the sort. Instead, he expects you to follow him, through sleight of hand, into the Manichaean world where Israeli violence is always virtuous and necessary, while Palestinian violence is always by definition sheer evil.

Palestinian scholar Rashid Khalidi, for one, clearly distinguishes between soldiers and civilians. In an interview in *The Drift* that took place two weeks after October 7, he argued explicitly against the claim of some student activists "that all Israelis are settlers, and therefore there are no civilians." Kirsch takes no notice of this interview but does briefly mention Khalidi at a handful of places in the book, mostly in order to mock his application of the settler colonial framework to Israel. He notably overlooks Khalidi's discussion, in *The Hundred Years' War on Palestine* (2020), of the Pakistani radical intellectual Eqbal Ahmad. A principled supporter of armed struggle in Algeria, Ahmad nonetheless criticized the PLO's use of violence on tactical grounds, arguing that armed struggle might not be the wisest course of action against Israel. Khalidi calls Ahmad's assessment "profound and devastating," and at the same time he credits Ahmad with having "shrewdly perceived the unique nature of the Israeli colonial project."

Eventually, however, Kirsch concedes that Khalidi "makes the crucial point that only a solution based on 'mutual acceptance' between Jews and Arabs can be morally acceptable," which Kirsch calls "the crucial dividing line between solutions, and advocates for those solutions, that can be called liberal and humane, and those that are dangerous and cruel." We are not supposed to notice that this concession invalidates the whole argument of the book. So much for Kirsch's central thesis about settler colonialism: that "the term itself is highly ideological," and therefore not just dangerous but genocidal.

ON SETTLER COLONIALISM is as unreliable and evasive as this throughout. The readings of scholarship are untrustworthy; when Kirsch says "in other words" after presenting an argument from a proponent of settler colonial studies, it is sometimes a struggle to see how his words resemble the ones he has quoted. For example, he cites political theorist Adam Dahl, whom he calls a "historian," arguing that the "settler colonial foundations of American democracy . . . continue to structure the basic features of modern democratic thought and politics," and then claims that "in other words," the United States is "illegitimately occupying land that rightfully belongs to Native Americans—and always will." Try as I might, I cannot find a property claim in this citation from Dahl. But even if Dahl does hold the view here attributed to him, what is most symptomatic in this example is Kirsch's refusal to engage the explicit claim of the text he cites. *Do* the main categories of American democratic thought continue to be socially and logically structured by the dispossession of Native Americans, or don't they? It doesn't seem to matter.

Kirsch does the same thing with the oft-cited dictum of the Australian anthropologist Patrick Wolfe that "invasion is a structure, not an event." Rather than dispute the contention, Kirsch prefers to diagnose it: settler colonialism "offers a political theory of original sin." Just as reactionaries before him claimed about communism, Kirsch wants to persuade us that here we have a case of secular radicals clamoring for the missing religion in their lives, unconsciously acting out Protestant, even specifically Calvinist, cultural scripts. All well and good—who among us hasn't known a leftist Puritan—but is Wolfe wrong, or is he right? Kirsch won't tell you. He writes as if you already assume Wolfe is wrong, so he doesn't have to argue it and can instead get by with explaining how anyone could come to think such a ludicrous thing. All this in what Walzer, whose scholarship is far more scrupulous than this, calls a "calm and careful" critique.

Further evidence of Kirsch simply dodging the claims of scholarship arises in his treatment of work by the Finnish historian Pekka Hämäläinen. In *Indigenous Continent: The Epic Contest for North*

America (2022), Hämäläinen claims that many Native peoples of North America had "opted for more horizontal, participatory, and egalitarian ways of being in the world." Kirsch calls the social and political arrangements of the eastern half of the continent a "slender evidentiary basis" for this claim, dismissing it as a "fable about the virtue and selflessness of Native Americans."

This is odd, first of all, because Hämäläinen is perhaps best known as the author of *The Comanche Empire* (2008), a book about vertical, exclusive, and hierarchical practices of Native nations in the southwest. He has never claimed that all Native Americans lived in stateless, non-hierarchical societies, only that many did. It is also odd because Hämäläinen is far from the only scholar to have reached similar conclusions. The historian Kathleen DuVal, for example, in her recent work *Native Nations: A Millennium in North America* (2024), assesses a long-standing debate on the question of whether great North American cities on the southern Aztec model, such as Cahokia near present-day St. Louis, were eventually abandoned and rejected for political reasons. She writes that they were: "The height of the great cities of Cahokia, Moundville, and the Huhugam can be seen as a golden age, but their descendants came to see it as a misguided era." In other words, just as Hämäläinen says, many eastern native North Americans experimented with hierarchical models of polity and found them unsatisfactory. They developed narratives about this experiment intended to prevent it from being reattempted. When Europeans, hailing from absolutist monarchical nation-states, encountered these natives, they simply assumed that they were incapable of achieving what seemed to them like the obviously best type of civilization. It was literally inconceivable to them—as, apparently, it remains for Kirsch—that a polity such as their own could have been attained and then later rejected.

A final method Kirsch employs to avoid directly engaging the central claims of settler colonial studies is to argue that accepting them would have negative consequences: "Indignation against past injustice is not a sufficient basis for remedying it.... it can easily become the source of new injustices." That may be true—and if it is, and you're paying more attention than Kirsch, you might notice that it could just as plausibly be leveled against countless actions of the State of Israel, including its response to October 7. Unfortunately, it resolves nothing about whether the basic claims of settler colonial studies are *true*. What matters, for Kirsch, is the turn—from the fact that it is "difficult to specify or even imagine" how one might decolonize the United States or Israel, to the claim that "on October 7, Hamas did more than imagine it."

A more generous response to an admitted failure of imagination would be to study and discuss what has been proposed so far. For example, many people and organizations are, right now, returning land to tribal governments. But the term "Land Back," the name for this movement, never appears in Kirsch's book. Perhaps that's because any consideration of real, practical steps to rectify or mitigate the colonial legacy would get in the way of his project: establishing a direct link between *any* claim about past and ongoing injustices and the specter of murdered and kidnapped civilians. When Kirsch briefly raises the idea of settler colonial societies ceding back parts of their territory and sovereignty to indigenous peoples, he treats the idea as an obviously utopian fantasy of radical scholars rather than as something that has in fact already taken place. Kirsch has the chutzpah to invoke the historian Roxanne Dunbar-Ortiz saying that "lack of imagination also indicates lack of commitment for figuring it out" and then proceeds to demonstrate just how correct she is through his own poverty of imagination. (Walzer cites this same passage in his review, seeming to think it applies to the wooly-headed utopians of settler colonial studies rather than to Kirsch and himself.)

I don't want to suggest that Kirsch scores no points at all. He is right that the habit among some activists of referring to the North American continent as "Turtle Island" can be ahistorical, homogenizing a creation story shared by specifically northeastern nations like the Lenape and Haudenosaunee into a generically "traditional," pan–Native American name for an anachronistically conceived geographical entity. He is also right that the now common ritual of placing "land acknowledgments" at the beginning of events and gatherings is often empty and hypocritical. But these points are not only irrelevant to his main argument; they are made by some of the very writers he spends pages criticizing. For example, Kirsch repeatedly criticizes Eve Tuck and K. Wayne Yang's 2012 article "Decolonization Is Not a Metaphor" for its academic language about "settler moves to innocence" and "settler futurity," with no mention of the fact that its central argument is precisely directed against shallow and hypocritical invocations of decolonial solidarity, including land acknowledgments. No one is more practiced in pointing out the foibles and follies of leftist subcultures than the left itself, but one rarely sees this acknowledged in polemics against the left. *On Settler Colonialism* is no exception.

A deeper issue that Kirsch touches on is the question of the implicit romanticism of some indigeneity discourse. When deployed glibly or thoughtlessly, the rhetoric of indigeneity—like the rhetoric of Zionism, for that matter—can sound like *Blut und Boden*: there are discrete parcels of land that are eternally granted by providence to equally discrete and eternally existing nations, and each nation belongs to its land in a quasi-mystical, ineffable relationship. On such an account, there is no place for nomads, migrants, or diasporas, and one can never truly belong to a place in which one's ancestors are not buried. This is a serious set of issues, and it is difficult if not impossible to square such a view with left-wing politics as typically understood. But Kirsch does not give this matter the attention it deserves, both because he fails to demonstrate that any of the thinkers he treats actually seriously hold views that resemble these and because he fails to acknowledge the extent to which Zionism, the ideological defense of which is this book's *raison d'être*, also operates on this set of assumptions. At one point, he alludes to this fact as a sort of gotcha—if scholars of setter colonialism love indigeneity so much, why aren't they Zionists?—but he can't have it both ways. Either this thinking is a problem, or it isn't, and Kirsch isn't honest enough to grapple with that.

EARLY IN the book, Kirsch makes the strange claim that because it has no practical applications, the framework of settler colonialism "has only a limited appeal to the people it claims to vindicate—

Native Americans." The only evidence he offers for this claim is that "mainstream advocacy groups like the National Congress of American Indians (NCAI) and the Native American Rights Fund do not use the language of settler colonialism or name decolonization as one of their aims."

This is like claiming that if a particular Black advocacy group, say the NAACP, doesn't use particular language or advocate a particular proposal—say, reallocating police budgets to social services—we should ignore that proposal's wide appeal to vocal civil rights activists elsewhere across the Black community. In other words, Kirsch simply assumes that "mainstream" groups speak for a majority—the flattering presumption of all those who style themselves as representatives of the mainstream, no doubt. And as it happens, the NCAI responded to the Vatican's 2023 repudiation of the "Doctrine of Discovery," which authorized the conquest of the Americas in the name of the Catholic Church, by saying that it hoped

> that today's announcement is more than mere words, but rather is the beginning of a full acknowledgement of the history of oppression and a full accounting of the legacies of colonialism—not just by the Roman Catholic Church, but by all the world governments that have used racism, prejudice and religious authority to not only justify past inequalities, but to allow, fuel, and perpetuate the institutionalization of those inequalities that continue to this very day.

Since Kirsch's evidence of Native American disinterest in settler colonialism is so weak, perhaps we can take a page from his book and ask why he makes this claim at all. Its purpose is quite obviously to persuade us that the preoccupations of settler colonial studies are those of guilty, privileged whites seeking absolution. Kirsch is honest enough to admit that "settler colonial studies does include Native activists and scholars," but he discounts them because "it is mainly an academic enterprise, and in 2021 Native Americans made up less than one half of one percent of university professors." (Read that again. What an interesting fact; perhaps there is a field of study that can account for this astonishing underrepresentation.) He approvingly cites a few Native scholars who do not use settler colonial frameworks and approaches, or who offer criticisms of the way some white scholars have deployed them. By contrast, he castigates a rainbow of scholars for their betrayal of the liberal narrative that America is always improving, and for believing that it would have been better if the colonization of the Americas had not taken place.

Kirsch positions himself carefully on the matter of U.S. history. At several points in the book, he invokes the triumphalist narrative according to which "the creation of the United States was a great and providential event." He acknowledges that this conservative history of heroes and explorers and martyrs for freedom could be credible "only so long as the country was defined solely by the experience of its white citizens." (Unsurprisingly, he makes no such acknowledgment in his potted history of Zionism, which is unreconstructed and pre-revisionist.) This bad old conservative history was then replaced, Kirsch tells us, with a liberal one according to which the United States only needed to make good on its founding promises, to become the country it had always claimed to be. This civil rights–era narrative, which Kirsch attributes to Martin Luther

King Jr. among others, was so popular that presidents from George W. Bush to Barack Obama have adopted it. Settler colonial studies is found guilty of abandoning it in favor of a Black Legend of a country born in the original sins of slavery and genocide, never to escape them.

Kirsch implicitly defends his repeated refusal to engage settler colonial studies at the level of its truth claims by dismissing it as having no practical political consequences. This is one of the functions of his assertion that it constitutes a "political theology" (as if political theology—and here we must surely count many a variety of Zionism—has never had practical political consequences!) and his insistence that the only possible outcome of "decolonization" is an unrealizable reversal of history or the mass disappearance of 7 million Israeli Jews and 300 million U.S. American settlers. Kirsch also uses this point to explain one of the most jarring disconnects in the book: If settler colonial studies produces an ideology that leads militant leftists to support the genocide of Jews in Palestine/Israel, why don't we see the same militance with respect to the settlers of the United States, Canada, Australia, and New Zealand?

On the surface, the settler colonial critique does exactly what proponents of the International Holocaust Remembrance Alliance definition of antisemitism want from critics of Israel: it doesn't single out Israel or hold it to a "double standard." What it says about Israel it says about the entire liberal Anglosphere. For Kirsch, however, this is not reassuring but rather an invitation to yet another ingenious sleight of hand. It is precisely because it is so hard to imagine decolonization in the United States and the other Anglosphere countries, he argues, that the ideology of settler colonialism seizes upon Israel. Because Israel was founded more recently and has a settler-native ratio closer to 1:1 than 9:1, it is easier for foolish militants, Kirsch alleges, to fantasize about its destruction and the genocide or expulsion of its settlers: Israeli Jews. (Never mind that here again he simply conflates decolonization with genocide and expulsion, treating their equivalence as a given.) But then he suggests—pulling the rug out from under his own observations about population size and founding date—that this differing treatment is fueled by antisemitism, making it possible for Israel to be "a country one could hate virtuously" since it is "home to a people whom Western civilization has traditionally considered it virtuous to hate." This is a truly impressive rhetorical feat, but it depends entirely upon the reader forgetting that Kirsch never actually establishes that the concept of settler colonialism must motivate genocidal hatred in the first place.

In reality, the radical left's narrative of U.S. history, like descriptions of Israel as colonial, long predated the rise of settler colonial studies in the academy. Kirsch hopes to shock us by observing that some scholars of settler colonialism, such as Mahmood Mamdani, contrast the Black liberal struggle for civil rights with the Native struggle for sovereignty. "When Black and Native aspirations are placed in opposition in this way," Kirsch writes, "it follows that, in seeking equality with white Americans, Blacks are embracing the guilt of the settler." Unfortunately for Kirsch's argument, this is no excess of settler colonial studies but a basic claim of Native activists, going back decades.

The Standing Rock Sioux activist and thinker Vine Deloria Jr., who served as executive director of the NCAI in the mid-1960s, devoted an entire chapter to this idea in his manifesto *Custer Died for Your Sins* (1969). Thirty years before Wolfe, in a book so practical it includes minute recommendations for reforms of bureaucratic practices in the Bureau of Indian Affairs, Deloria wrote of the "unthoughtful Johnny-come-lately liberal who ... generally defines the goals of all groups by the way he understands what he wants for the blacks." Deloria defends the decision of Native movements to avoid the March on Washington, explaining that the civil rights movement confused Indians, who "could not believe that blacks wanted to be the same as whites." But Stokely Carmichael and Black Power made sense to them, he writes, because they spoke in terms of self-determination:

> Indians had understood when Carmichael talked about racial and national integrity and the need for fine distinctions to be made between white and black. But when King began to indiscriminately lump together as one all minority communities on the basis of their economic status, Indians became extremely suspicious. The real issue for Indians—tribal existence within the homeland reservation—appeared to have been completely ignored.

And so it remains, with Kirsch ventriloquizing Native peoples' supposed rejection of settler colonial studies on their behalf.

But let me not be evasive myself. Suppose Kirsch grants that U.S. history is, in fact, a vale of tears—a catastrophe continually piling wreckage at the feet of the angel of history, in the resonant image of Walter Benjamin that he critiques in his final chapter. Still, might Kirsch be right that it is politically unwise to dwell on this truth?

He is not the first liberal to think so. This was the thesis of pragmatist philosopher Richard Rorty, who defended it nearly thirty years ago in *Achieving Our Country: Leftist Thought in Twentieth-Century America* (1998). "Those who hope to persuade a nation to exert itself," Rorty wrote, "need to remind their country of what it can take pride in as well as what it should be ashamed of." Even in those halcyon days prior to settler colonial studies, Rorty was worried about "a widespread sense that national pride is no longer appropriate." The culprits then were Foucault and Heidegger. Their readers—the "academic left"—wound up viewing the United States "as something we must hope will be replaced, as soon as possible, by something utterly different." Like Kirsch, Rorty saw a quasi-religious drive at work; the anti-patriots, he said, "think of themselves as a saving remnant."

In contrast to this "wrong kind of despair," Kirsch concludes his book by offering the Talmudic concept of *ye'ush*, or despair over a lost object. According to Jewish law, we must be willing to give up on "perfect justice," in the following sense: someone whose property is stolen, then purchased by a third party unaware of the crime, cannot demand it back from the buyer, though the victim remains "entitled to monetary compensation and damages." The same is true of nations, lands, and history, Kirsch urges. Attempting to restore the past can only result in new wrongs; the best we can do is muddle forward, resigning ourselves to loss.

Yet here Kirsch might have taken more of a cue from his predecessor. He and Rorty both sound the classic liberal theme of imperfection, but where Kirsch stresses resignation, Rorty stresses achievement, quoting William James: "Democracy is a kind of religion, and we are bound not to admit its failure. Faiths and utopias are the noblest exercise of human reason, and no one with a spark of reason in him will sit down fatalistically before the croaker's picture." In one way or another, Kirsch spends much of his book chastising radicals for abandoning the liberal "arc of justice" narrative, but here he seems to relinquish it himself, failing to muster one iota of Rorty's democratic optimism. Instead, through the example of Kazuo Ishiguro's novel *The Buried Giant*, in which characters are put under a "spell of oblivion," Kirsch invites us to forget and move on.

A strenuously secular thinker, Rorty opposed his account of cruelty to religious notions of sin. As I have argued elsewhere, however, his view comports perfectly well with the Jewish conception of *teshuva*, or repentance: turning away from sin to forgiveness and redemption, which necessarily includes making restitution to the extent possible. Perhaps *teshuva*, then, is the Jewish concept Kirsch should have reached for. *Ye'ush*, as Kirsch counsels it, is a comfort to the powerful rather than the afflicted. *Teshuva* demands more.

But can a nation do *teshuva*? This is one of the oldest and deepest questions of Judaism. The traditional answer, coming down to us through the prophets and rabbis, is yes. This cuts against Kirsch's cynical reading of settler colonial studies, which he portrays as committed to "mak[ing] hundreds of millions of 'settlers' disappear" or nothing. In fact, the literature of Indigenous studies and Native American studies, whether identifying as part of settler colonial studies or not, is full of inspiring and promising examples of activists using every legal, cultural, and political means at their disposal to pursue decolonization.

In *Indigenous Economics: Sustaining Peoples and their Lands* (2022), for example, Salish-Kootenai economist Ronald L. Trosper writes of how in 2015, the Navajo, Ute Mountain Ute, Uintah and Ouray Ute, Hopi, and Zuni nations formed a coalition to protect 1.3 million acres of land in southeastern Utah by creating the Bears Ears National Monument in an innovative application of the 1906 Antiquities Act—a move Potawatomi botanist and writer Robin Wall Kimmerer (hardly anyone's idea of a decolonial militant) recently called "a transformative step toward healing a long history of colonial taking." President Obama signed a proclamation to this effect, though he kept decision-making authority in the hands of the U.S. government rather than consent to the co-management structure the tribes had proposed. President Trump then attempted to reduce the size of the monument to 200,000 acres, in accordance with the wishes of the Utah congressional delegation and state legislature (as well as a private uranium-mining company). The tribes initiated legal action, which remains in limbo, but in 2021 President Biden reinstated the monument at greater than its original size.

Perhaps this all falls into the category of what Kirsch calls "defending tribal rights, enforcing treaties, and holding government accountable—concrete goals that can be achieved within the framework of American law." But it is a mistake to conclude that groups pursuing such resolutions "fail to see that the colonial relationship endures"—another view advanced by Mamdani that Kirsch attempts to use as a *reductio* of settler colonial studies. (In this case, I take issue with Mamdani's view, but that is no reason to reject his whole body of work.) For one thing, this and other instances of "Land Back" often involve highly innovative legal strategies, including pursuing legal personhood for tracts of land and bodies of water, as in the cases of Te Urewera and Te Awa Tupua in New Zealand—upending the Anglo-settler legal system in order to make it possible to recognize the relationship described in the title of Dana Lloyd's book *Land Is Kin* (2023). For another, as evidenced by the Bears Ears example, these cases remain contentious. They provide clear evidence of a political divide between forces who seek to perpetuate, deepen, and consolidate the colonial pattern and those who seek to stall, frustrate, or even reverse it.

There are moments in *On Settler Colonialism* when it seems as though Kirsch is ready to acknowledge that the intellectual framework of settler colonialism does not inevitably lead to genocidal violence. He admits, for example, that "Western intellectuals seldom openly endorse the eliminationist ambitions of either Jews or Arabs, and the leading ideologues of settler colonialism do not call for Israelis to be pushed into the sea." He mentions, in this regard, Mamdani's support for a one-state solution and Lorenzo Veracini's support for two states as a first step toward a longer-term resolution. And yet, Kirsch simply waves these explicit arguments away with the contention that the "actual effect of the ideology of settler colonialism is not to encourage any of these solutions. It is to cultivate hatred of those designated as settlers and to inspire hope for their disappearance." This extreme pitting of denotation against connotation, at the conclusion of his book, cries out for nothing so much as diagnosis.

On Settler Colonialism begins with a pledge: See this trendy body of scholarship? It's not what it appears to be! It moves on to the turn: making settler colonial studies disappear by evading its central truth claims in favor of too-clever diagnosis. Knowing this, Kirsch hopes, will be enough for credulous audiences (including, apparently, Michael Walzer) to satisfy themselves. As Caine says in his monologue about the turn: "Now you're looking for the secret, but you won't find it, because of course you're not really looking. You don't really want to know. You want to be fooled." For the prestige, Kirsch brings settler colonialism back, as "the ideology of settler colonialism," a repository of everything that liberals, centrists, and conservatives have hated about radical academia since McCarthyism—too secular and too religious at the same time, both anti-American and anti-Jewish, both ineffectual and dangerous, both genocidal and disrespectful of genocide. The trick is done, and now you can clap.

But even if "settler colonialism" goes the way of "critical race theory," becoming the new pet hate of liberal pundits' anti-academic screeds and conservative politicians' draconian legislation, the phenomenon itself will remain. Getting rid of "settler colonialism" will not stop people from seeking to address the ongoing and enduring injustices of colonization, any more than getting rid of "critical race theory" will make everyone unaware of the vast differences in life outcomes across differently racialized populations. As I write, Gaza has been destroyed and far-right Israeli politicians have developed plans to resettle it. Uncounted numbers of Palestinian men, women, and children lie dead or live starving. Instead of obsessing over how to make the apparently ineffable mystery of opposition to this cruelty and criminality disappear, the real magic would be devoting some imagination to care, repentance, and repair.

CONTRIBUTORS

Joelle M. Abi-Rached is Associate Professor of Medicine at the American University of Beirut and the author of *Asfūriyyeh: A History of Madness, Modernity, and War in the Middle East.*

Aaron Bady is a writer in Oakland and editor at *Stanford Social Innovation Review*. His writing has also appeared in *The Nation, The New Yorker,* and *The New Inquiry.*

Gianpaolo Baiocchi is Professor of Sociology at NYU, where he directs the Urban Democracy Lab. His latest book is *We, the Sovereign.*

Samuel Hayim Brody is Assistant Professor of Religious Studies at the University of Kansas and author of *Martin Buber's Theopolitics.*

Noura Erakat is a human rights attorney, Associate Professor at Rutgers University, New Brunswick, and author of *Justice for Some: Law and the Question of Palestine*. Her writing has also appeared in *The Nation* and *Jadaliyya.*

Janice Fine is Professor of Labor Studies and Employment Relations at Rutgers School of Management and Labor Relations and director of its Workplace Justice Lab. Her writing has also appeared in *The Nation.*

Robin D. G. Kelley is Gary B. Nash Professor of American History at UCLA and a contributing editor at *Boston Review*. His many books include *Freedom Dreams: The Black Radical Imagination.*

Jeanne Morefield is Associate Professor of Political Theory and Fellow at New College, Oxford and a Non-Resident Fellow at the Quincy Institute for Responsible Statecraft. Her latest book is *Unsettling the World: Edward Said and Political Theory.*

Benjamin Schlesinger is a national union staff member who worked on turnout and persuasion efforts during the 2024 election season.

Mark Schmitt is Senior Director of the Political Reform Program at New America. He was previously executive editor of *The American Prospect.*

Marshall Steinbaum is Assistant Professor of Economics at the University of Utah and Senior Fellow at the Jain Family Institute. His writing has also appeared in *Phenomenal World*, *The American Prospect*, and *Current Affairs*.

David Austin Walsh is a historian and author of *Taking America Back: The Conservative Movement and the Far Right*.